Business Process of Banking
Vol. III

Corporate Credit
CMS
Trade Finance
Foreign Exchange
Treasury

Sunil Aggarwal

First Edition: January 2021

Disclaimer:

Every possible effort has been made to ensure that the information contained in this book is accurate at the time of going to press. The Author does accept responsibility for any errors or omissions, however caused. No responsibility for loss or damage occasioned to any person acting, or refraining from action, as a result of the material in this publication will be accepted by the Author.

REVIEW FROM EXPERTS

An excellent effort. Banking over the last three decades has evolved substantially. Certain segments of banking are currently world class providing global leadership - in particular payment systems. The book has covered the complex, wide ranging subject in a holistic manner. Since the industry itself is evolving dynamically on a continuous basis, there is no doubt that there would be need to frequently update the book. Nevertheless, a monumental effort.

P.H. Ravikumar
Chairman, Utkarsh Small Finance Bank

Sunil is a reservoir of banking knowledge. He has worked and delivered at senior positions in public and private sector banks, particularly, in operations, credit and technology implementation. For the last 35 years I have known him to be a meticulous and thorough professional. Many times, we invited him to deliver a talk on 'Banking in Technology' at IIT Roorkee. I am sure the readers will find the book immensely useful.

Vinay K. Nangia
Professor & Head (Rtd.)
Department of Management Studies
IIT Roorkee

It would be a great book for someone looking to enter banking or putting down their roots in it.

Vijay Mani
Partner, Deloitte India Consulting

Rarely does one come across such a holistic view of banking processes. I believe this book is an excellent map for anyone who wishes to begin exploring the depths of an Indian banking operation. It can undoubtedly prove invaluable to students, software designers and to anyone who wishes to embark on a banking career.

Rajan Ghotgalkar
Former Country Head - India
Principal Financial Group

Sunil's book is culmination of his extraordinary commercial banking journey. Sunil comes from that rare breed of commercial bankers who have soiled their hands in all areas of commercial banking in large public and private sector (both old and newgen) banks and have also handled successful consulting assignments. He has exceptionally strong foundation in commercial banking operation and IT system covering both retail, corporate banking and trade businesses. The book is different from conventional books on banking. It will come handy to all practicing bankers as it is like a practice manual covering all areas of banking at one place where one can dip into. The book is voluminous but the coverage & contents merit the volume.

SKV Srinivasan
Former Executive Director, IDBI Bank Ltd.

Book on Business Process & IT Systems in Indian Banks by Mr. Sunil Aggarwal is one of the finest books covering all the important aspects of banking system. The book covers most of the topics needed to understand in the banking system. It is amazing how Mr. Aggarwal has managed to capture even the minutest point relevant to over banking eco-system. I would highly recommend the book to all those who want to learn about Indian banking system as it has been written by a practitioner. It is hard to get wealth of information provided by the book on various aspects and application of technology in banking operations. Well written book. My sincere compliments to Mr. Aggarwal for sharing his knowledge and documenting nuances of banking in this book.

Sanjay Sharma
Co-founder & Group Chief Ops & Digital Officer
APAC Financial Services Pvt. Ltd.

I am honored to write this foreword for Sunil Aggarwal & his 'wonder book'. Sunil has a unique way of breaking down complexities into simple facts with ease of comprehension. This book brings the world of banking to the common man's understanding. In my banking experience, I have not come across such a detailed manuscript that has eloquently narrated banking practices – all in one place. It is a refresher for Bankers & a treasure trove to the rest. Happy reading!

Rebecca Rocque
Consulting SME in BFSI industry

ABOUT THE AUTHOR

Sunil has over 36 years' experience in banking in the areas of Corporate Banking, Core Banking System, Branch Management, Banking Operations, Operations Risk & Fraud Control, Rehabilitation & Recovery, Branch Expansion and writing manuals.

Sunil was Vice President in IDBI Bank for 10 years. He was Head Branch Operations, overseeing operations over 500 branches. Prior to that, he was Vice President in ICICI Bank for 2 years and was Chief Manager in Bank of India where he served for over 23 years. Besides, he worked in an Investment Management Company as Director and CEO of its Indian subsidiary.

Sunil holds the distinction of heading the first branch of ICICI Bank as well as IDBI Bank in New Delhi. In IDBI Bank he co-headed the Project for implementation of Core Banking Solution.

Sunil is a rank holder commerce graduate from Delhi University and a Certified Associate of Indian Institute of Bankers. He has been a Visiting Faculty/Guest Speaker at prominent management institutes.

Sunil is now a freelance Consultant engaged in training, education and implementation of technology projects relating to banking and finance. Key consultancy projects include:

- Senior Advisor for 2 years with Deloitte Consulting in its project for setting up India Post Payments Bank.
- Consultant with a premier Government of Germany's development organization in its project with

NABARD for introduction of Kisan Credit Card Solutions in co-operative banks. Sunil authored Reference Guide for on-boarding Kisan Credit Card and the Handbook on Mobile Banking.

- Financial Planning Project of an Asset Management Company. Besides setting up the software application, he wrote User Manual.
- Wrote Manual on Business Process of Banking for a leading BFSI Software Company for its software professionals.
- Conducted Enterprise Risk Assessment Study for a Bank in Dubai.
- Prepared financial model of a European Union aided project for a prominent infrastructure consultancy company.

PREFACE

During the last two decades, banking in India has undergone a paradigm shift. From 'paper-based branch banking' it has morphed into 'Anywhere Anytime Banking'. Information Technology has played the key role. To manage these fast-paced disruptions, Regulations, Business Practices and Processes have been redefined, realigned and put in place afresh altogether. Large investments have been made in technology infrastructure for leveraging these opportunities created by the advent of IT in the Banking Sector.

The comprehension of these developments has, however, not kept pace at the required level amongst various stakeholders. For example, bankers need better understanding of IT related issues. On the other hand, IT professionals require better domain knowledge about banking practices and processes. Similarly, students of banking need more inputs on practical aspects of banking than the theory.

These gaps have increased operational risks for the banks as well as for the customers This book is an attempt to address this issue. The Book describes commonly followed Practices & Business Processes of banking in India. It does not cover subjects such as credit appraisal, processing of credit proposals, assessment of working capital requirements, management of different types of risks, agriculture credit, micro-banking, etc.

The Book consists of three Volumes as described below:

<u>Volume I:</u> Regulations, Operations, Digital Banking and IT infrastructure.

<u>Volume II:</u> Customer Acquisition, Deposits, Retail Loans, Credit Card, Third Party Product Services and Customer Service.

<u>Volume III:</u> Corporate Credit, Trade Finance, CMS, Foreign Exchange and Treasury.

The book will be useful to all stakeholders – IT Professionals, Bankers, Students as well as Customers. Since it is focused on processes for doing business, IT Professionals will get required insight into the banking domain. Banking students will get to know about the practical aspects of banking. This will help them in becoming "Job-ready". Bankers, in pursuit of horizontal extension of their knowledge, will find it of immense benefit as it provides concise overview of various verticals of banking.

The narration is precise and straightforward, with suitable illustrations wherever necessary. While I have attempted to include up to date information, in the dynamic and fast-paced environment, it is quite possible that some changes may occur by the time the book reaches you. Future trends point out to more disruptions happening sooner than later. RBI has already introduced "Regulatory Sandbox" to hasten the process of innovation. It is therefore imperative that we all keep in close touch with the developments on an ongoing basis to keep ourselves updated periodically.

Contents

FOREIGN EXCHANGE

CHAPTER 1
CORPORATE CREDIT

I. INTRODUCTION

Banks are catering to all sections of the society for all types of financial services – be in accepting deposits, financing or facilitating collection/payments. The activities are broadly categorized in to Retail Banking and Business Banking. While Retail Banking relates to non-commercial activities, Business Banking is for commercial activities; irrespective of the type of legal entity i.e., whether the activity is being carried out by individuals, firms or companies.

The financing of commercial activity falls under the Asset category of Business Banking. While professionals like doctors, architects, chartered accountants, lawyers, normally carry out the activity in their individual capacity; most of the other business activity is under other legal structures like proprietorship/partnership firms, companies, societies etc.

Promoters of business require funds to set up and expand their business. Banks are important vehicle for pooling small savings for funding these businesses. Without such financial support from banks, the businesses would find it very difficult to grow. On the other hand, without such demand from the businesses, banks would not find enough avenues to invest the amount collected from depositors. Business Banking Assets therefore form a very significant and critical source of business.

Banking Assets are primarily created by funding fixed capital and working capital requirements of a business. The fixed capital requirements comprise funding of fixed assets such as:

- Land & Building
- Plant & Machinery
- Other fixed assets like furniture/fixture, vehicles, office equipment etc.
- Pre-operative expenses
- Margin money for working capital

Typical financial structure of a Project

Fixed Cost of the Project (including margin money for working capital)	Promoter's Equity (40 to 50%) Term Loan from the bank (50 to 60%)
Working Capital	Margin money (25%) Working Capital Limits from the bank (75%)

The financing of these items by banks is by way of Loan. The Loan is disbursed at the time of acquiring these fixed assets, mostly by paying directly to the vendors/suppliers. The Loan could be for all or any of the aforesaid fixed assets. It could be for setting up a business or for buying any specific asset later on or even for meeting some short term requirement which is not necessarily for buying an asset. The repayment of the loan is over a period in installments out of the income accruing in future.

While the acquiring of fixed assets is financed by way of loan from the bank, the funds required to meeting working capital requirements is funded by banks by way of cash credit. The working capital requirement is for items like:

- Raw Material
- Wages
- Consumables
- Power
- Fuel
- Selling Expenses
- Salary/Administrative expenses

The working capital cycle starts from the point when expenses for manufacturing/operating start and ends when the sales proceeds are received. All the funds required till that time are called working capital funds. Banks set up Cash Credit limit based on the requirement.

The illustration below, in respect of a manufacturing company, would explain the aforesaid:

a	Time required to procure raw material from the suppliers	20 days
b	Time required to procure consumables from the suppliers	30 days
c	Time required to convert raw material in to finished goods	15 days

d	Time required to sell the finished goods after manufacturing	30 days
e	Time required to receive payment from the buyer of the finished goods	45 days
f	Minimum quantity required to be manufactured for sale	10 days
g	Total number of days	150 days

It means that the investment required for running the manufacturing cycle would be equivalent of investment in each of the aforesaid segments for the defined days before the money started getting recycled in to the business. The minimum quantity of manufactured goods required to make a saleable lot (item vi above) is to be accounted for not only procurement of raw material but also for the cost of manufacturing the finished goods and the finished goods inventory. The total value thus arrived at is the amount of working capital required.

This working capital requirement is funded by:

- Owner's contribution
- Credit received from the raw material supplier
- Bank finance

While the total Bank finance available is broadly calculated as above, the availability of limit is generally regulated through allocating limit against each of the item – raw material, finished goods and receivables.

The aforesaid is a very simple illustration of a typical working capital cycle. There are several other components under each category. However, the fundamentals remain the same i.e., all necessary requirements to operate any business other than investment in fixed assets (like land, building, plant and machinery) are considered as working capital requirements; which are funded by own capital, market credit and bank finance.

The working capital limits are granted by way of Cash Credit, DA LC facilities and Bills Purchase/ Discounted.

Banks offer wide range of fund based and non-fund based products and services to all sectors of business – large, medium and small sectors operating in different segments viz., manufacturing, trading, services, international/ domestic etc. Key products and services under business banking are described below:

II. PRODUCTS

i) Fund based Products

The products which involve lending of bank's funds are known as funded products. The main products under this category are:

a. Loans

Medium and Long Term Loans – for financing medium/ long term needs like purchase of fixed assets and margin money for working capital

Short Term Loans – for financing small capital expenditure/short term working capital gap

- Loan is not an operating account with deposits and withdrawals. It is an account from where amount is disbursed, either in lump sum or in installments, either directly to a vendor or in to the operating account of the borrower.

- Loan could be for a short period (say 6 months) or for long period (6-7 years).

- Banks also provide working capital term loan to meet company's working capital requirements which are not covered under normal cash credit facility either because the working capital gap is in excess of norms or long term nature of requirement or also when the amount is required to be repaid in a defined time schedule.

- Loan is repaid installments or in lump sum as per agreed terms. Mostly the installments are uniform, principal loan amount equally divided into number of monthly/quarterly/half yearly installments. Interest is repayable separately on actual basis.

- The interest is charged at the end of the month on the basis of day-end balances during the month. The interest is to be repaid immediately. In some cases, particularly relating to new projects, the recovery of interest may be after an agreed period of moratorium, depending upon projected period from when the income would start generating. Normally in such cases, the interest is compounded at quarterly intervals.

- The interest is charged either at a fixed rate or on floating rate, linked to the Base Rate of the bank.

- Mostly, short term loans are on fixed rates and medium/long term loans are linked to Base Rate.

- Banks charge penal interest, usually 2% per annum, on the overdue amount of installment as well as interest.

- The primary security for the loan is the asset purchased with the said loan amount. In case of clean loan, there is no primary security.

- In case of movable property like plant/machinery, vehicle (which are removable), the security is created by way of hypothecation for which the Deed of Hypothecation is executed by the borrower in favor of the bank.

- In case of immovable property like land and building, the security is the mortgage of the said property. The mortgage is mostly by way of equitable mortgage which does not require execution and registration of mortgage deed.

- At times, apart from charge on primary security, the bank creates charge on other properties of the borrower which is called 'collateral security'.

b. **Cash Credit**

- Cash Credit, as the name suggests, is the credit given in cash for day to day working capital requirement of the borrower.

- It is an operating account wherein the borrower frequently deposits and withdraws amount as per his day-to-day requirements.

- The bank fixes a limit up to which the borrower can withdraw the amount.

- The limit is assessed at the time of appraisal and sanction of working capital facility and is usually valid for 1 year. After 1 year, the requirement is reviewed and the limit is reduced or increased depending upon the performance of the borrower and estimated requirement for the next year.

- The security for the cash credit facility is the floating charge on the current assets.

- While entire current assets are charged to the bank as security, the primary security is the current asset (like raw material, semi-finished & finished goods, consumables, receivables etc.) i.e., the core items which the borrower produces/manufactures or deals in.

- Bank arrives at a Drawing Power for each month based on the value of primary security less required margin and also estimated requirement during the month, within the over-all sanctioned limit.

- The Drawing Power for the month is set up for each month in the beginning. The borrower is required to restrict his balance within the said Drawing Power.

- Interest is charged on the basis of day-end balance and is debited/recovered at the end of every month.

- Banks charge penal interest, which is usually 2% per annum on the balance in excess of the Drawing Power for the month. The borrower is expected to repay the excess amount immediately.

c. Packing Credit

- Packing credit is the working capital finance for exporters. It is provided against confirmed export order(s) for procurement of material/manufacturing of the material, solely for export against the confirmed order.

- The advance is recovered by the bank from the sales proceeds of the exported goods.

- The exporter is required to submit the order/export letter of credit to the bank against which packing credit is to be disbursed.

- Exporter has to submit the export documents to the bank within the shipment date so that the bank purchases/discounts/negotiated the bill, recovers packing credit and send the bill to the importer's bank for payment.

- The rate of interest is much lower than the normal working capital finance from the bank.

- If exporter fails to export and submit documents in stipulated time, bank recovers the amount and interest with penalty.

- In case the exporter receives a Red clause Letter of Credit, packing credit or any other working capital finance is not required for export of the said goods as the issuing bank authorizes the exporter's bank to provide funds at issuing bank's risks and responsibility. The exporter's bank recovers the advance from the LC Issuing Bank.

d. Overdraft

- Overdraft is an operating account, similar to Cash Credit.

- Overdraft is also granted in current account to meet short term requirement.

- When the advance is either clean or against financial assets like Fixed Deposit, NSC, Bonds, shares etc., it is granted by way of Overdraft. On the other hand, Cash Credit is against core current assets like raw material, semi-finished and finished goods and receivables.

- Overdraft facility is meant for day to day requirement wherein the customer frequently deposits and withdraws amount.

- The bank fixes a limit up to which the borrower can withdraw the amount.

- The limit is assessed at the time of appraisal and sanction of working capital facility and is usually valid for 1 year. After 1 year, the requirement is reviewed and the limit is reduced or increased depending upon the available security and customer's need.

- The security for the overdraft facility is the pledge of the Security.

- Bank arrives at a Drawing Power based on the value of primary security less required margin, within the over-all sanctioned limit. The borrower is required to restrict his balance within the said Drawing Power.

- The balance in overdraft accounts may fluctuate between debit and credit. Overdraft is an efficient form of borrowing as interest is paid only when money is withdrawn. It gives flexibility to deposit money into the account any time to reduce the outstanding balance or to withdraw money whenever needed as long as the amount does not exceed the limit. Interest is calculated daily on the end of the day outstanding balance and is normally charged at the end of each month.

- Banks also consider Overdraft for a short period on ad hoc basis (without elaborate assessment) to meet urgent needs of the customer having current account. The facility is granted by permitting the customer to overdraw.

- Interest is linked to the Base Rate of the bank

- Interest is charged on the basis of day-end balance and is debited/recovered at the end of every month.

- Banks charge penal interest, which is usually 2% per annum on the balance in excess of the Drawing Power for the month.

e. **Domestic Bills Purchase/Bill Discounting**

Business is all about sales of goods and services. The sales transaction between two business entities is usually on continuing basis where the payment, unlike retail sales, is not made in cash. If the seller and the buyer are located in different cities, even when there is no credit period, there is a gap of 10-15 days between delivery of goods and payment thereof. Over and above this, if goods are sold on credit, the over-all cycle of sales proceeds further increases.

The seller is often interested in replenishing his investment as quickly as possible. Therefore, he approaches his bank to pay against these outstanding bills. The bank purchases/discounts the said sales bills, levies charges/commission and interest for the period of credit. Upon receipt of the payment from the buyer within the agreed period, the bank settles the transaction. If the payment is not received from the buyer, the bank recovers the dues from the seller.

Simple Transaction Flow

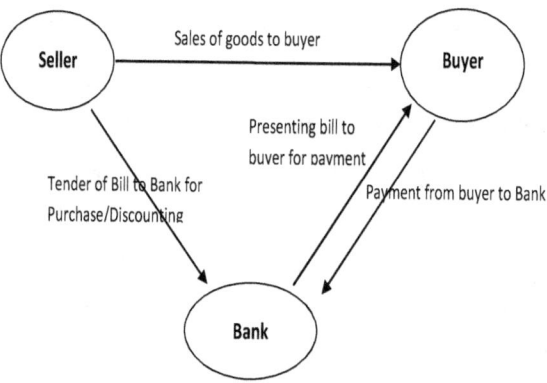

Types of Bills Purchase/Bills Discounting

i) <u>DP Bills Purchase (Documentary)</u>

When the seller tenders the bill to the bank for purchase, it is accompanied by the Transport Receipt for the goods. If the bill is payable on demand (i.e., without any credit period), the buyer pays the amount to the bank and gets the Transport Receipt along with other documents, duly discharged by the bank in favor of the buyer. The buyer takes delivery of the goods from the Transporter after producing the discharged transport receipt. This type of bank transaction is known as DP Bills Purchase.

ii) DA Bills Purchase (Documentary)

If the bill is payable after a certain specified period from the date of receipt of documents by the buyer, the buyer gets the aforesaid transport receipt and the documents after recording his acceptance to pay on due date. The due date is calculated adding credit period to the date on which acceptance was recorded. The buyer pays the amount on the due date. At times, the due date is pre-decided irrespective of the date on which the buyer receives the documents. All these bills where buyer retires the documents from the bank after recording his acceptance are known as DA Bills Purchase.

iii) Clean Bills Purchase

In addition to the aforesaid 2 types of bills purchase, banks also provide facility of purchasing bills which are not backed by any transport receipt. The seller and the buyer are directly receiving goods and the seller provides a copy of the invoice to the bank for purchase. Bank provides immediate funds to the seller and the buyer makes payment to the bank as per contract. Bank adjusts the purchase amount, interest, charges etc., from such payment.

iv) Bills Discounting

In this case, the delivery of the goods/services directly takes place between the seller and the buyer and in exchange the seller receives acceptance from the buyer for payment of the amount on due date. The seller thereafter tenders the bill to the bank for discounting. The bank pays the amount to the seller and presents the documents to the buyer on due date for payment. In other words, bank discounts the bill before it is due and pays the amount to the customer after deducting discount for the unexpired period. The transaction is practically an advance against the security of the bill and the discount represents the interest on the advance from the date of purchase of the bill until it is due for payment. The past track record and reputation of the drawee are taken into consideration for taking decision to discount the bill.

Bank keeps a margin of 5-10 per cent i.e., lends 90-95 per cent of the amount receivable from the buyer. Out of this margin amount, bank recovers interest, charges etc., and pays balance amount to the seller.

f.   Forex Bills Purchase/Discount/Negotiation

When the sale is to another country, bills for such sale are presented by the customer for collection, purchase or discounting. If it is only for collection, there is no element of financing. When it is submitted for purchase/discounting, as explained above under Domestic Bills Purchase/Discounting, the bank either purchases the bill or discounts it, depending upon the nature of bill. Mostly, the bills are for purchase since they are not as yet accepted for payment or are sight bills (demand bill - payable on presentation).

Bank purchases the bill and sends it to its correspondent bank in that country for presenting to the bank of the importer. The bill contains, inter-alia, shipment bill issued by the shipping company/airlines. If it is a sight bill (demand bill), the payment is released immediately. However, if it is a usance bill (payable after certain number of days), the documents are released upon acceptance by the importer. On due date, the payment is received by the customer who recovers bill purchase amount and interest/charges etc. Balance amount is paid to the customer.

Very often, export (the customer of the bank), receives Letter of Credit (LC) from the importer's bank which takes upon itself responsibility of payment of the bill (on demand or on due date, as the case may be) if the exporter or its bank tenders required documents within stipulated time period. Since the payment is assured by the importer's bank, exporters always look for LC. Exporter's bank also feels more secured and therefore prefers this. The financing of such bills (tendered under LC) is called "negotiation of bill". Exporter's bank negotiates the documents, provides funds to the exporter immediately and submits the documents to the importer's bank for payment. The transactions are conducted under the rules framed by International Chamber of Commerce (Uniform Customs and Practice for Documentary Credits – UCP 600) by banks engaged in international banking. It is important however that LCs contain suitable reference to the said Rules.

Sometimes, the documents are not submitted in accordance with the terms and conditions mentioned in the LC. In such cases, banks hold back release of funds (negotiation under reserve) pending confirmation from importer's bank. Negotiation of documents under LC is a very popular form of funding of post-shipment finance and banks are willing to extend this facility with far less level of credit assessment/due diligence.

g. Channel Financing

Banks finance suppliers of goods to the company (bank's customer) against their receivables from the company. After supply of the goods to the company of the bank, suppliers submit to the bank, bills drawn on and accepted by the company, payable after stipulated period.

Banks discount these bills and pay to the suppliers proceeds after deducting interest/charges and margin. The margin amount is released upon recovery of the amount on due date from the company after deducting unrecovered interest/charges (if any).

This helps the company in providing down payment for its purchases which enables it to get better price. The suppliers get their receivables financed easily at competitive price. Banks are able to increase business on the strength of its known customer (the company).

h. Distributor Finance

Banks finance distributors of the company (bank's customer) to meet their working capital requirement against security of the goods supplied by the company. Banks manage collections from distribution channels which helps reducing company's effort in tracking each receivable and reconciliation is considerably. It also helps the bank in controlling company's receivables against which it may have financed. Banks verify the credit worthiness of the distributors before setting up limit.

This facility also helps companies managing their receivables easily since banks are able to track sales realization. The distributors gain in terms of easy finance on better terms than what are available to traders if they get bank finance independently. Banks are able to extend their reach on the strength of the company. Thus, it is a win-win proposition for all.

i. Foreign Currency Loans

Banks also arrange foreign currency loans for its customers to finance short/ medium term requirements in foreign currency. Many multinational banks, as well as Indian banks having foreign currency deposits/resources, provide this facility. The customer is required to repay the loan in the same currency in which the loan was taken.

At the time of taking loan, the foreign currency is converted into Indian Rupees at the prevailing rate and equivalent rupees are lent to the customer. At the time of repayment, the customer is required to buy required amount of foreign currency at the rates prevailing at that point of time. The exchange rate fluctuation has to be borne by the customer. If the customer is an exporter and earns foreign currency, he may repay the loan from the foreign exchange earnings, thus avoiding exchange rate fluctuations/conversion charges.

Depending upon the interest rates in India vis-a-vis other countries, customer sometime prefers to take loan in foreign currency. The loan could be from his bank in India or from the bank located outside. Apart from prevailing interest rates, the decision also depends upon (a) Expectation of exchange rate movements in future (b) Foreign Exchange earnings of the customer (c) Interest Rate ceiling stipulated by RBI.

For example, the interest rate in India on loans is around 12% p.a. The US dollar interest rates in US may be around 5% p.a. Assuming that this rate is within interest rate ceiling stipulated by RBI, the customer borrows 10,00,000 US dollars for repayment after 3 years. The exchange rate at present is Rs.45 per dollar. After 3 years, at the time of repayment, if the exchange rate is Rs.48/- per dollar, the net outflow of amount would be as under:

- Loan Amount Received = 10,00,000 X 45
  = 4,50,00,000

- Interest on Loan for 3 years = 5% X 3 i.e., 15%
  = 1,50,000 (simple rate assumed for illustration)

- Total amount (dollars) repayable after 3 years
  = 11,50,000

- Total Indian Rupees @ 48 per dollar = 11,50,000 X 48 = 5,52,00,000

- Actual interest in Indian Rupees for 3 years
  = 1,02,00,000 (5,52,00,000 – 4,50,00,000)

- Effective Rate of Interest
  1,02,00,000/3)/4,50,00,000% = 7.56% p.a.

If the exchange rate of rupee strengthens cost of a dollar becomes less than Rs.45/-, the effective rate would be less than contracted rate of 5%.

ii) Non Funded

These products do not require lending of funds by the bank. Bank extends its credibility support to the business for facilitating business transactions. Main products under this category are –

a. Guarantees

A bank guarantee is an irrevocable commitment by the issuing bank to make a payment, at the request of its client, to the beneficiary specified in the bank guarantee, subject to the beneficiary filing a request with the bank to that end.

There are certain key elements which are pre-requisite for a bank guarantee. They are –

- The guarantee is only in terms of a clearly specified amount payable by the bank. It does not involve any other type of liability for the bank (non-financial);

- The guarantee has a certain specific expiry date and a period thereafter within which the beneficiary has right to claim the amount. Upon expiry of the claim period, all rights of the benefit cease to exist;

- The guarantee though refers to the contract between the customer of the bank and the beneficiary, the payment obligation of the bank is totally unqualified;

- Bank has no right to hold back payment of the amount of guarantee irrespective of its ability to receive consent of the customer or recovery of the amount from the customer;

- The customer (on whose behalf bank issued the guarantee) has no right to stop payment of the guarantee amount if demanded by the beneficiary;

- The customer can take up the dispute (if any) to court and obtain court order restraining payment. Only in that event the payment can be held back before release of the same by the bank.

Bank issues guarantees on behalf of its customers in favor of their clients for various purposes like –

- To secure advance paid by a buyer to a seller to enable the seller to meet expenses to manufacture/procure goods and supply to the buyer. In case the supplier is unable to supply the goods as per terms of the contract, the buyer is entitled to invoke the guarantee to recover the amount of advance;

- To submit tender without paying the required earnest money. In lieu of earnest money, the guarantee is generally accepted;

- To seek delivery of the items by the transporter without upfront submission of goods receipt with a commitment to submit the goods receipt as and when received. The transporter is entitled to invoke the guarantee in case it suffers any loss on account of this;

- To assure the quality of performance of the plant/equipment supplied to the user by the manufacturer. In case the performance is not as per terms of contract, the user can invoke the guarantee;

- To secure payment of the cost of plant/machinery in installments in future buyer provides guarantee to the supplier. On default, the supplier is entitled to invoke the guarantee to recover the dues

Purpose

Based on the purpose, guarantees are sub-divided into following categories:

i) Financial Guarantee

To substitute money are financial guarantees. For example:

- Advance Payment Guarantee to secure advance received by the customer

- Bid Bond (in lieu of Earnest Money)

- Deferred Payment Guarantee

- Shipping Guarantees issued by a bank to a carrier to be used in lieu of submitting original negotiable Bill of Lading.

ii) Performance Guarantee

To secure specific performance by the customer or his product, guarantee is provided by the supplier. For example:

Guarantee to a purchaser of a machinery on behalf of the machinery manufacturer for satisfactory performance of the machinery. In case of unsatisfactory performance, the buyer is entitled to demand payment of money specified under the guarantee.

Security

Banks may or may not take security (cash or otherwise) for issuing the guarantees. Accordingly, the guarantees are categorized as "Clean" of "Secured" Guarantees.

Key Regulatory Guidelines

RBI has issued guidelines to the banks for issuing guarantees, key points whereof are given below:

- As regards the purpose of the guarantee, as a general rule, the banks should confine themselves to the provision of financial guarantees and exercise due caution with regard to performance guarantee business.

- As regards maturity, as a rule, banks should guarantee shorter maturities and leave longer maturities to be guaranteed by other institutions.

- No bank guarantee should normally have a maturity of more than 10 years. However, in view of the changed scenario of the banking industry where banks extend long term loans for periods longer than 10 years for various projects, it has been decided to allow banks to also issue guarantees for periods beyond 10 years.

- Banks should adopt the following precautions while issuing guarantees on behalf of their customers.

- As a rule, banks should avoid giving unsecured guarantees in large amounts and for medium and long-term periods. They should avoid undue concentration of such unsecured guarantee commitments to particular groups of customers and/or trades.

- Unsecured guarantees on account of any individual constituent should be limited to a reasonable proportion of the bank's total unsecured guarantees. Guarantees on behalf of an individual should also bear a reasonable proportion to the constituent's equity.

- In exceptional cases, banks may give deferred payment guarantees on an unsecured basis for modest amounts to first class customers who have entered into deferred payment arrangements in consonance with Government policy.

- Guarantees executed on behalf of any individual constituent, or a group of constituents, should be subject to the prescribed exposure norms.

- It is essential to realize that guarantees contain inherent risks and that it would not be in the bank's interest or in the public interest, generally, to encourage parties to over-extend their commitments and embark upon enterprises solely relying on the easy availability of guarantee facilities.

At the time of issuing the guarantee, bank creates liability in the books as under:

Debit : Customer's Liability for Guarantee Issue

Credit: Bank's Liability for Guarantee Issue

The Liability is reflected as an off balance sheet item and is reversed upon payment of the guarantee or after the expiry of the claim period of the guarantee and receipt of original guarantee/release letter by the beneficiary.

b. Letter of Credit

It is issued by the bank on behalf of its customers in favor of the vendor undertaking to make the payment as per agreed terms upon submission of specified documents by the vendor in respect of the deal.

Upon issuance of Letter of Credit, the Buyer's bank replaces its own credit worthiness to that of the Buyer, it undertakes to reimburse the Seller for the value of the Letter of Credit "Irrevocably" provided two underline conditions are fulfilled by the Seller:

- All the documents stated in the LC are presented;

- All the terms and conditions of the LC are complied with.

It is named a Letter because initially the LCs were issued manually in a Letter format address by Issuing Bank to Beneficiary confirming its conditional undertaking to reimburse the Beneficiary, the amount of the LC provided above 2 basic conditions are fulfilled.

LCs deal with documents only and are mostly governed by Uniform Customs and Practice for Documentary Credits – UCP 600 framed by the International Chamber of Commerce.

The beauty of the LC is that if above two conditions are fulfilled, Issuing Bank will effect payment to the Beneficiary, irrespective of Applicant reimburses the Issuing Bank or not. Thus, a Letter of Credit is an undertaking issued by a bank in favor of a Beneficiary

(Seller), which substitutes the bank's creditworthiness for that of the Applicant (Buyer).

LCs are issued for domestic purchases as well as for import. The import LCs have to be compliant of provisions for import of goods & services and foreign exchange management laws of the country.

Explanation

In trade, the buyer and the seller, located in different locations, may not know each other and hence the seller may have problem in ascertaining credit worthiness of the buyer. On the other hand, the buyer may not have comfort on seller's worthiness to get advance payment or payment against un-inspected and un-delivered goods. To overcome this barrier, they agree for a modus operandi under which the buyer stipulates inspection and dispatch of the goods through reliable sources and provides his bank's assurance to the seller on submission of the documents evidencing aforesaid within the stipulated time. The seller gets payment from the buyer's bank (or his correspondent/advising bank) once he submits the required documents, without any condition. The only conditions are with respect to submission of the stipulated documents strictly as mentioned. This takes care of concerns of both, buyer and the seller.

Process Flow

- The Applicant is the Buyer that arranges for the LC to be issued.

- The Beneficiary is the Seller named in the LC in whose favor the letter of credit is issued.

- The Issuing or Opening Bank is the Buyer's (applicant) bank that issues or opens the LC favor of the beneficiary and substitutes its creditworthiness for that of the Buyer.

- An Advising Bank may be named in the LC to advise the beneficiary about the LC. The role of the Advising Bank is limited to establish apparent authenticity of the advised LC.

- The Paying Bank is the bank nominated in the LC that makes payment to the beneficiary (it can be Advising Bank also), after determining that the submitted documents conform to the terms of LC. The Issuing Bank advises the Paying Bank the procedure for getting the reimbursement of the amount (paid by it to the Beneficiary) from the Issuing Bank directly or through another intermediary bank nominated by the Issuing Bank.

- The Confirming Bank is the bank, which, under instruction from the Issuing Bank, substitutes its creditworthiness in place of for that of the issuing bank. It takes up responsibility to pay to the Seller directly irrespective of Issuing Bank's ability to pay.

Benefits of Letter of Credit

- The beneficiary is assured of payment as long as it complies with the terms and conditions of the letter of credit. The credit risk is transferred from the applicant to the issuing bank.

- The beneficiary is able to avoid country risk by seeking confirmation from a bank in his own country.

- The buyer is able to buy the goods as per his specifications, duly inspected/certified by his agent in seller's country and dispatch through goods carriers of his choice.

- The buyer is able get credit from the seller based on credit worthiness of his bank.

Risks involved in Letter of Credit

- Since all the parties involved in Letter of Credit deal with the documents and not with the goods, the risk of Beneficiary not shipping goods as mentioned in the LC is still remains though buyer seeks to overcome this by getting the goods inspected by his local agent/ representative.

- The Letter of Credit as a payment method is costlier than other methods of payment

- The Beneficiary's documents must strictly comply with the terms and conditions of the Letter of Credit for Issuing Bank to make the payment. The documents are exposed to the risk of rejection if any discrepancy is found in documents.

LCs are also used as means of finance when the goods are purchased on credit (D/A LCs). The documents received under the LC are delivered against acceptance of the customer of the LC opening bank (buyer) and the payment is made after the expiry of the credit period. The buyer is thus able to have his working capital requirement funded through LC to the extent of value of the purchased goods for the period of credit. On due date, bank pays to the seller and recovers the amount from the customer (the buyer).

The operating part of LC is discussed in the details in the Trade Finance chapter hereinafter.

III.   SECURITY

Most of the financing by banks to the business is on secured basis. The security may be of the assets financed or some other assets. The banks define these securities as under:

i)   Primary Security

The asset for which the bank lends the money is called the "Primary" security. For example, if the loan is for construction of factory building, the "Primary" security would be the building. Similarly, if the loan is for purchase of machinery, the "Primary "security would be the machinery. In case of working capital finance (e.g., cash credit), the "Primary" security would be the stock of goods in trade – raw material, semi-finished/finished goods etc. If the facility is bills purchase, the "Primary" security would be the goods, deliverable to the buyer upon payment.

ii)   Collateral Security

The collateral security is the charge on assets other than for which the money has been lent. For example, the bank may create charge on the land/building of the company as collateral security for the cash credit facility given to it (although there is no loan for land/building).

iii)   Lien

Banks have a right of lien (which is known as Banker's Lien) on the amount payable to a person (outstanding balances in deposit accounts).

The right can be exercised only if there is a crystallized liability as on the date of exercise of lien and amounts.

The right is confined to security / properties in the bank's custody.

A banker cannot exercise lien on money or deposit given for a specific purpose and also in respect of Trust Accounts.

Banker can exercise its right of lien, even in case of time barred debts also as this being enforced by itself, without intervention of court.

iv) Insurance

Banks obtain insurance cover for loan assets against risks of theft, burglary, damage on account of fire, riots, strikes, earthquakes, floods etc.

A suitable clause is incorporated in the policy for payment of insurance claim directly to the bank.

v)   Margin

Bank stipulates margin for all forms of secured lending. It means that the customer should provide a certain percentage of money from his own sources for purchasing an asset. For example, a margin of 25% for purchasing a machine costing Rs. 10 lacs would mean, the customer should contribute Rs.2.5 lac and balance Rs.7.5 lac would be the loan amount from the bank. This margin applies in all forms of secured lending, be it loan, and cash credit, overdraft or bills purchase/discounting. The margin percentage would vary in each case. In case of unsecured loan, the margin is not applicable in the absence of security on which the margin is calculated.

After reducing margin from the value of the security, Drawing Power (or Drawing Limit) is derived, not exceeding sanctioned limit, up to which the customer is allowed to avail the finance.

For example:

Sanctioned Limit	Value of Security	Margin	Power after deduction of margin	Drawing	Actual available Drawing Limit
10,00,000	20,00,000	25%	15,00,000	10,00,000
10,00,000	12,00,000	25%	9,00,000	9,00,000

IV. CREATION OF SECURITY

It depends upon the type of asset and the governing laws. Banks have to follow the process defined under the laws so that, in case of need, banks are able to take recourse to legal action to enforce their charge for recovery of the dues. Explained below are various means for creation of charge on different types of assets:

i) Immovable Property

Immovable property is defined as the property which is not movable; for example, land, building, machinery embedded to the ground and hence a part & parcel of the land/building. The charge on the immovable property is created by way of mortgage. The owner of the property continues to remain in possession of the mortgaged property and use the property till the mortgagor takes legal recourse to enforce mortgage rights.

Mortgage is created, primarily by the following 2 methods:

Equitable Mortgage

Every land/building has its unique identity. The owner is either a person who is holding title deed or is a person who has inherited the property from their ancestors (and hence does not hold any title deed). The title deed is the document, registered with the Registrar of Assurances, evidencing ownership of the property. If the owner is holding such registered title deed, the equitable mortgage can be created by that person.

For creating equitable mortgage, the person (mortgagor) has to deposit the title deeds with the mortgagee (bank in this case) with the purpose of creating bank's charge on the property. There is no written document of mortgage and there is no requirement of registration. This is the most prevalent form of creation of mortgage as it is very convenient and cost effective

This type of mortgage is not possible where the owner does not hold title deed.

Registered Mortgage:

The owners not holding title deeds and where for some other reasons registered mortgage is considered necessary, a mortgage deed is required to be executed by the owner in favor of the mortgagee. This mortgage deed is registered with the Registrar of Assurances. It attracts higher stamp duty but gives more effective proof of creation of charge. This is not very common as it is costly as well as time consuming.

These securities cannot be enforced without intervention of the court. Sec 69 of transfer of Property Act stipulates that mortgaged property cannot be sold without intervention of court.

Only in case of English Mortgage subject to conditions mentioned therein, it is possible to sell the property thereunder without intervention of court, which is rare in Indian conditions.

ii) Movable Property

Hypothecation Charge

- Charge on movable property like goods, machinery, furniture, equipment etc., is generally created by banks by way of "hypothecation".

- "Hypothecation" means a charge in or upon any movable property, existing or future, created by a borrower in favor of a secured creditor without delivery of possession of the movable property to such creditor, as a security for financial assistance and includes floating charge and crystallization of such charge into fixed charge on movable property.

- The owner is required to execute a deed of hypothecation in favor of the bank creating charge in its favor which entitles the bank to take possession of the movable property, sell it and recover its dues in case of default, after following due legal process. The legal process requires the bank to seek court orders before taking such action.

- Hypothecation is an extended idea of pledge, but the possession of the property will remain with the borrower.

- The owner of the movable property continues to enjoy all rights on the property till enforcement of rights by the lender as provided in the hypothecation deed through legal recourse. Since the hypothecation rights are floating on the goods in trade, the owner is well within his rights to buy and sell these goods until so restrained through legal means.

- Once possession of goods is taken by secured creditor i.e., by way of seizure then the goods can be dealt like pledged goods. As per law only peaceful possession is permitted and force cannot be used

Pledge

- In case of pledge, goods are in possession of the bank and with prior notice pledged goods can be sold to realize banks overdues.

- Bankers can exercise their rights on the properties which are in their custody, owned by the borrower.

iii) Financial Assets

Those financial assets like shares, bonds, savings certificates, life insurance policies etc., which are transferable/assignable in favor of third parties, can be taken as security. While some of these securities are transferable, others (like life insurance policy) are only assignable. Each of these securities has its own laid down process for creation of charge. For example, shares being in de-materialized form, the charge are created by registration with the Depository (NSDL/CDSL). The charge on NSC/Insurance Policy is registered by the issuing authority requires endorsement on the document.

Owner executes pledge agreement in favor of the bank, authorizing it to encash the security on default.

In case of lending against bank's own fixed deposit, bank takes a simple letter of lien and appropriation along with discharged fixed deposit receipt. This entitles the bank to appropriate the proceeds of the fixed deposit on default or on maturity.

V. DOCUMENTATION & DISBURSEMENT

i) Documentation

It includes –

- Verification of titles to the immovable property –

  Search in the office of the Registrar is done to trace the chain of ownership linking down to the present owner

- Verification of ownership of all movable and immovable properties –

  Ascertain whether any charge already exists in favor of any other bank/person. In case the customer is limited company, the search in the office of the Registrar of Companies (ROC) is carried out. All charges on the assets of the company are required to be registered in the records of ROC and therefore the search would reveal all existing charges

- KYC of the customer and the guarantor(s)

- Verification of Memorandum and Articles of Association (MOA) of the company (if the customer is a company) to ensure that the purpose of borrowing is within the stated objects of the company and the articles of association have requisite proviso for directors to borrow. In case of societies and trusts, their incorporation deeds are scrutinized to ensure this.

- Resolution of the Board of Directors/Managing Committee, as per proviso of the MOA/Deed of Incorporation, authorizing officials to execute documents on its behalf

- Execution of documents – by the authorized officials in favor of the bank, containing agreement terms, hypothecation/pledge/mortgage etc.

- Filing of charge in the ROC in case of limited companies

ii) <u>Disbursement</u>

- In case of cash credit and overdraft, an operating account is opened wherein limit is set up based on security, margin, and sanctioned limit. Customer is provided with the cheque book to draw cheques in favor of business clients as per terms of sanction.

- In case of loan, the amount is released directly to the vendors for the assets to be purchased. There may be variations but the disbursement has to ensure that the funds released are utilized for the purpose for which loan has been sanctioned.

- In case of bills purchase/discounting, the amount is released upon submission of bills from time to time. The amount so released is reduced from the sanctioned limit to arrive at available limit for subsequent bills. As and when purchased/discounted bills are paid, the available limit is increased, not exceeding sanctioned limit.

VI.   REVIEW

i)   Periodic Review

Most of the facilities, including loan for 5-7 years, are reviewed yearly. The review involves study of over-all performance of the unit, payment history, value of security, future projections etc.

The operations in the account are reviewed periodically to not only ensure that the interest and installments are being paid in time but also to ensure that the value of security is as proposed. Also, the financials of the business entity are scrutinized quarterly to see whether the unit is performing satisfactorily. Bank officials periodically visit the working place of the unit to make an on the spot assessment. In case of cash credit limit, monthly statement of stocks is also taken from the unit and scrutinized.

ii)   Ad hoc Review/Revision of limit

Ad hoc review/revision is undertaken either when the borrower approaches bank for review before completion of the year due to unforeseen situation or the bank finds some abnormal situation which warrants immediate review. Banks do revise limits during such ad hoc review to meet such emergent situations to protect the interest of the unit and the bank.

VII.   REHABILITATION

The continuation of bank's facilities depends upon timely repayment of installments and interest, which in turn depends upon performance of the business. If there are continuing losses in the business, it loses its capacity to meet its obligations towards, inter-alia, repayment of bank dues and interest. The value of security, particularly in regard to current assets, starts diminishing. Banks have legal rights to recall the advance and enforce the security in case of default. However, this may generally prove counter-productive as the assets are generally unable to fetch real market value when sold in distress. Moreover, there is every possibility that the losses so being suffered by the company are due to some short term conditions. It may also be that the company was suffering more due to financial deficit and/or bottlenecks in production which could be resolved by providing timely assistance in overcoming the shortcomings. All these reasons and many more, therefore require a comprehensive review of the situation and analysis of the real causes of company going into sickness. If there is a scope to resuscitate the unit through restructuring of financial assistance/additional funding, the banks draw rehabilitation plan.

Many times, banks are unable to take timely action or the view point of the bank is different from the management of the company. To resolve such cases, based on the extent of loss that a company has already suffered, the cases are referred to Board for Industrial & Financial

Reconstruction (BIFR). It is a statutory body formed by the Government of India in the year 1985 to look in to such cases. Given below is the brief introduction of BIFR:

- The Government of India enacted a special legislation namely, the Sick Industrial Companies (Special Provisions) Act, 1985 (1 of 1986) commonly known as the SICA. The main objective of SICA is to determine sickness and expedite the revival of potentially viable units or closure of unviable units.

- The Board of experts named the Board for Industrial and Financial Reconstruction (BIFR) was set up in January, 1987 with a view to securing the timely detection of sick and potential sick companies owning industrial undertakings, the speedy determination by a body of experts of the preventive, ameliorative, remedial and other measure which need to be taken with respect to such companies and the expeditious enforcement of the measures so determined and for matters connected therewith or incidental thereto. Those measures are to be taken by a body of experts in the (a) Legal (b) Financial restructuring and (c) Managerial areas.

- SICA applies to companies both in public and private sectors owning industrial undertakings:

  - pertaining to industries specified in the First Schedule to the Industries (Development and Regulation) Act, 1951, (IDR Act) except the industries relating to ships and other vessels drawn by power and;

- Not being "small scale industrial undertakings or ancillary industrial undertakings" as defined in Section 3(j) of the IDR Act.

- The criteria to determine sickness in an industrial company are –

  o the accumulated losses of the company to be equal to or more than its net worth i.e., its paid up capital plus its free reserves

  o the company should have completed five years after incorporation under the Companies Act, 1956

  o It should have 50 or more workers on any day of the 12 months preceding the end of the financial year with reference to which sickness is claimed.

  o It should have a factory license.

Prudential Framework for Resolution of Stressed Assets

Subsequently RBI issued directives putting in place directions with a view to providing a framework for early recognition, reporting and time bound resolution of stressed assets, called the Reserve Bank of India (Prudential Framework for Resolution of Stressed Assets) Directions 2019 applicable to:

- Scheduled Commercial Banks (excluding Regional Rural Banks);

- All India Term Financial Institutions (NABARD, NHB, EXIM Bank, and SIDBI);

- Small Finance Banks; and,

- Systemically Important Non-Deposit taking Non-Banking Financial Companies (NBFC-ND-SI) and Deposit taking Non-Banking Financial Companies (NBFC-D).

With exception of cases relating to -

- Restructuring in respect of projects under implementation involving deferment of date of commencement of commercial operations (DCCO)

- Revival and rehabilitation of MSMEs

- Restructuring of loans in the event of a natural calamity and for borrower entities in respect of which specific instructions have already been issued or are issued by the Reserve Bank to the banks for initiation of insolvency proceedings under the IBC

The Framework contains directions with regard to:

a. Early identification and reporting of stress

b. Implementation of Resolution Plan

c. Implementation Conditions for Resolution Plan

d. Delayed Implementation of Resolution Plan

e. Prudential Norms

Any action by lenders with an intent to conceal the actual status of accounts or evergreen the stressed accounts, are subjected to stringent supervisory / enforcement actions as deemed appropriate by the Reserve Bank, including, but not limited to, higher provisioning on such accounts and monetary penalties.

Lenders are required to make appropriate disclosures in their financial statements

VIII. RECOVERY

Bank may resort to foreclosure if:

- the repayment is not as per agreed schedule

- the mortgaged property is found deficient in terms of title or value

- the bonafide of the customer is found doubtful

- the customer's death

- the performance of the business is severely adverse, jeopardizing the safety of the money lent by the bank

- If the rehabilitation is not possible or has failed to yield the desired results, banks take recourse to recovery action

- any other event turns out to be in contravention of the agreed terms

If the follow up action does not result in improvement, banks recall the advance as per proviso of the agreement by issuing legal notice. Banks usually have legal rights to pursue borrowers as well as guarantors to recover the dues from their personal assets. To sell the assets taken as security and/or to recover dues from the personal assets of the borrowers/guarantors, banks have to approach court of law. The case is handed over to the empaneled lawyer for filing suit in the court of law to recover the dues, obtain permission to acquire and sell the security to recover the dues.

Many a times, the legal rigmarole severely restricts banks rights and unduly delays/forestalls the recovery of the dues. This results in unwarranted losses to the banks.

Securitization and Reconstruction of Financial Assets and Enforcement of Security Interest Act, 2002 (SARFAESI)

To regulate securitization and reconstruction of financial assets and enforcement of security interest and for matters connected therewith or incidental thereto, the Government of India enacted SARFAESI Act in the year 2002.

SARFAESI empowers Banks / Financial Institutions to recover their non-performing assets without the intervention of the Court. The key provisions of the Act are:

i)   The provisions of this Act are applicable only for NPA loans with outstanding above Rs. 1.00 lac.

ii) NPA loan accounts where the amount is less than 20% of the principal and interest are not eligible to be dealt with under this Act.

iii) Non-performing assets should be backed by securities charged to the Bank by way of hypothecation or mortgage or assignment.

iv) Security Interest by way of Lien, pledge, hire purchase and lease not liable for attachment under Sec.60 of CPC, are not covered under this Act.

v)   The act gives the following powers to the affected Banks:

   • To issue demand notice to the defaulting borrower and guarantor, calling upon them to discharge their dues in full within 60 days from the date of the notice.

- To give notice to any person who has acquired any of the secured assets from the borrower to surrender the same to the Bank.

- To ask any debtor of the borrower to pay any sum due or becoming due to the borrower.

vi) Any Security Interest created over Agricultural Land cannot be proceeded with.

vii) If on receipt of demand notice, the borrower makes any representation or raises any objection, Authorized Officer shall consider such representation or objection carefully and if he comes to the conclusion that such representation or objection is not acceptable or tenable, he shall communicate the reasons for non-acceptance Within One Week of receipt of such representation or objection.

viii) A borrower / guarantor aggrieved by the action of the Bank can file an appeal with DRT and then with DRAT, but not with any civil court. The borrower / guarantor has to deposit 50% of the dues before an appeal with DRAT.

ix) If the borrower fails to comply with the notice, the Bank may take recourse to one or more of the following measures:

- Take possession of the security
- Sale or lease or assign the right over the security
- Manage the same or appoint any person to manage the same

x) The Act provides three alternative methods for recovery of non-performing assets -

- Securitization
- Asset Reconstruction
- Enforcement of Security without the intervention of the Court

xi) Notwithstanding anything contained in section 69 or section 69A of the Transfer of Property Act, 1882 (4 of 1882), any security interest created in favor of any secured creditor may be enforced, without the intervention of court or tribunal, by such creditor in accordance with the provisions of this Act.

xii) Reserve Bank of India issued guidelines and directions to banks for appropriate action in this regard.

Banks are also exploring the other avenues of recovery, which are enumerated below:

- <u>Recovery through Lok Adalats:</u>

  Under this system borrowers can admit the liability to a Bank and express intention of settlement through a compromise deal.

- <u>Recovery through Debt Recovery Tribunals (DRTs):</u>

  This is available in respect of Rs.10 lacs and above. Banks can file A Recovery application in the Tribunal. The process of disposal of the recovery proceedings is quicker unlike in general courts. However, after enactment of the SARFAESI, banks prefer that instead of taking recourse in DRTs.

- Compromise Settlements:

  This is the latest trend amongst back to go by this route to get rid of hard core NPAs. This process does not involve any interference of courts. A settlement is arrived by bank accepting reduced amount of repayment. This is done to avoid delays in following normal legal course of action which involves costs and time.

- One Time Settlement Schemes (OTS):

  Helps in recovery of large amounts through compromise.

- Legal action through Courts:

  Filing suit in courts for recovery of dues. It is a long drawn process and is the last option of the bank.

Insolvency and Bankruptcy Code, 2016

The legal and institutional machinery for dealing with debt default, either through the Indian Contract Act, 1872 or through special laws such as the Recovery of Debts Due to Banks and Financial Institutions Act, 1993 and the Securitization and Reconstruction of Financial Assets and Enforcement of Security Interest (SARFAESI) Act, 2002 did not however yield effective results. Action through the Sick Industrial Companies (Special Provisions) Act, 1985 and the winding up provisions of the Companies Act, 1956 also neither aided prompt recovery by lenders nor swift restructuring of indebted firms.

To improve the situation, the IBC, 2016 was enacted in May 2016. It became single law to deal with insolvency and bankruptcy by consolidating and amending various laws relating to re-organization and insolvency resolution. It covers individuals, companies, limited liability partnerships, partnership firms and other legal entities as notified (except financial service providers) and is aimed at creating an overarching framework to facilitate the winding up of business or engineering a turnaround or exit.

The IBC aims at insolvency resolution in a time-bound manner (180 days, extendable by another 90 days under certain circumstances) undertaken by insolvency professionals.

Salient Features of IBC, 2016

The institutional infrastructure under the IBC, 2016 rests on four pillars, viz.,

- **First Pillar: Insolvency Professionals**

  They are a class of regulated persons who assist in the completion of insolvency resolution, liquidation and bankruptcy proceedings. They are governed by 'Insolvency Professional Agencies', who will develop professional standards and code of ethics as first level regulators.

- **Second Pillar: Information utilities**

  This is institutional infrastructure which collects, collates, authenticates and disseminates financial information. It maintains electronic data bases on lenders and terms of lending, thereby eliminating delays and disputes when a default actually takes place.

- **Third Pillar: Adjudicating authorities**

  They are National Company Law Tribunal (NCLT) and Debt Recovery Tribunal (DRT), the institutions where adjudication takes place. NCLT is the forum where cases relating to insolvency of corporate persons are heard. DRT is for insolvency proceedings related to individuals and partnership firms. These institutions have their Appellate bodies, viz., the National Company Law Appellate Tribunal (NCLAT) and the Debt Recovery Appellate Tribunal (DRAT), respectively.

- **Fourth Pillar: Insolvency and Bankruptcy Board of India**

  This body has regulatory oversight over insolvency professionals, insolvency professional agencies and information utilities.

Under the provisions of the Code, insolvency resolution can be triggered at the first instance of default and the process of insolvency resolution has to be completed within the stipulated time limit.

For individuals, the Code provides for two distinct processes, namely, "Fresh Start" and "Insolvency Resolution", and lays down the eligibility criteria for these processes. The Code also establishes a fund (the Insolvency and Bankruptcy Fund of India) for the purposes of insolvency resolution, liquidation and bankruptcy of persons. A default-based test for entry into the insolvency resolution process permits quick intervention when the corporate debtor shows early signs of financial distress.

On the distribution of proceeds from the sale of assets, the first priority is accorded to the costs of insolvency resolution and liquidation, followed by the secured debt together with workmen's dues for the preceding 24 months. Central and State Governments' dues are ranked lower in priority. The code proposes a paradigm shift from the existing 'debtor in possession' to a 'creditor in control' regime. Priority accorded to secured creditors is advantageous for entities such as banks.

When a company defaults on its debt, control shifts from the shareholders / promoters to a Committee of Creditors to evaluate proposals from various players about resuscitating the company or taking it into liquidation. This avoids the delays (under the Sick Industrial Companies Act) which often led to erosion in the value of the company.

In order to further strengthen the insolvency resolution process, the Government brought in amendments which provide for prohibition of certain persons from submitting a resolution plan and specifies certain additional requirements for submission and consideration of the resolution plan before its approval by the committee of creditors.

IX.   PROVISIONING FOR NPAs

RBI has laid down detailed guidelines for income recognition, assets classification and provisioning. The guidelines, known as IRAC (Income Recognition and Asset Classification) comprehensively cover different sectors, types of facilities, securities etc., and therefore it is difficult to draw any uniform snapshot. However, broadly the guidelines are summarized below:

i)   If the due amount is outstanding for more than 90 days, the loan is deemed as NPA and categorized as "sub-standard" category.

ii) If the default period increases to one year, the loan is shifted to "doubtful" category.

iii) If any Loan is considered unrecoverable for any reason, the same is categorized under "loss".

iv) Banks are required to make provisions for loss in their books based on the category of NPA, period of default and availability of security as per guidelines issued by RBI as referred to above.

v)   As soon as a Loan is categorized as "NPA", the entire amount of unrecovered interest and other charges are to be reversed and are not to be booked henceforth.

vi) If one account of a borrower has been classified as NPA, all other accounts would also be required to be classified as NPA irrespective of their 'overdue' position.

vii) However, banks may continue to record such accrued interest in a Memorandum Account in their books. For the purpose of computing Gross Advances, interest recorded in the Memorandum account should not be taken into account.

viii) If interest is computed in an NPA account and transferred to Interest Suspense Account, the balance in the said Interest Suspense Account needs to be reduced from the total loan outstanding to arrive at net position.

ix) Interest realized on NPAs to be taken to income account provided the credits in the accounts towards interest are not out of fresh/ additional credit facilities sanctioned to the borrower concerned.

x) If arrears of interest and principal are paid by the borrower in the case of loan accounts classified as NPAs, the account is no longer be treated as NPA and may be classified as 'standard' accounts. With regard to up-gradation of a restructured/ rescheduled account which is classified as NPA, further guidelines are contained in the circular.

xi) A general provision varying between 0.25 to 1.00 percent is required to be made in the case of standard assets, depending upon the sectors so defined by the RBI.

xii) On Sub-Standard Assets, provision is made for 10% of the Unsecured portion of outstanding amount

xiii) On Doubtful Assets, provision of 20 to 50 percent of unsecured portion of the outstanding is to be made depending upon overdue period

xiv) On Loss Assets, 100% of the outstanding amount is to be provided for.

The guidelines for categorization of assets as NPA and income recognition norms in respect thereof vary from time to time and are different in each country.

CHAPTER 2
TRADE FINANCE

Trade Finance in banks typically deals with banking activities for trade between buyer and the seller. These activities involve bank's interaction between their customer (buyer or seller) and the counter party. Banks have various liability and asset products like bills collection, bills purchase/discounting, guarantee, letter of credit and packing credit etc. to cater to these activities. Packing Credit, though not directly involves connecting with the buyer, is closely linked to a confirmed order or letter of credit which is issued by the buyer and therefore it is covered under Trade Finance.

Other business activities of customers like manufacturing, processing and storing etc. do not require bank's inter-face with the buyer and therefore they are outside "Trade Finance" segment of banks. These other activities are catered to by banks through various liability and asset products like current account, cash credit account, overdraft account etc.

Trade finance facilitates trade by helping overcome the information asymmetry between buyers and sellers, enabling them to trust a system whereby sellers will be paid under certain conditions and buyers will get the products they paid for. Trade finance contributes to international trade in four areas – (i) payment facilitation (ii) risk mitigation (iii) financing and (iv) provision of information about the status of payments or shipments. Every trade finance transaction involves some combination of these four elements, adjusted to suit the circumstances of a particular market or of a trading relationship.

Trade finance is the lifeline of trade because more than 90% of trade transactions involve some form of credit, insurance or guarantee.

Key Trade Finance products and services provided by banks are:

- Letter of Credit
- Bills Negotiation under LC
- Bills Purchase/Bills Discounting
- Bills Collection
- Packing Credit
- Guarantee
- Foreign Exchange Transactions (other than trade)

I. LETTER OF CREDIT (LC)

As explained in the Section for Letter of Credit in the Business Banking Chapter, an LC is a letter issued by a bank on behalf of a buyer of goods/services (its customer) in favor of the vendor irrevocably undertaking to reimburse the Seller the value mentioned in the LC provided the documents stated in the LC are presented and all the terms and conditions of the LC are complied with. LC deals with documents only and is independent of the terms of the underlying trade. The undertaking is unconditional except for the submission of the documents strictly as mentioned in the LC. To remove ambiguity about the role and responsibility of each party, the International Chamber of Commerce has formulated standard rules known as Uniform Customs and Practice for Documentary Credits – UCP (UCPDC 600) which are binding to all – banks and parties to the LC. LCs contain suitable clause in this respect.

LCs are issued for domestic purchases as well as for import. The Terminology mentioned in the following paragraphs is explained below:

- The Applicant is the Buyer that arranges for the LC to be issued.

- The Beneficiary is the Seller named in the LC in whose favor the letter of credit is issued.

- The Issuing or Opening Bank is the Buyer's (applicant) bank that issues or opens the LC favor of the beneficiary and substitutes its creditworthiness for that of the Buyer.

- An Advising Bank may be named in the LC to advise the beneficiary about the LC. The role of the Advising Bank is limited to establish apparent authenticity of the advised LC.

- The Paying Bank is the bank nominated in the LC that makes payment to the beneficiary (it can be Advising Bank also), after determining that the submitted documents conform to the terms of LC. The Issuing Bank advises the Paying Bank the procedure for getting the reimbursement of the amount (paid by it to the Beneficiary) from the Issuing Bank directly or through another intermediary bank nominated by the Issuing Bank.

- The Confirming Bank is the bank, which, under instruction from the Issuing Bank, substitutes its creditworthiness in place of for that of the issuing bank. It takes up responsibility to pay to the Seller directly irrespective of Issuing Bank's ability to pay.

- The Nominated Bank is the bank which is nominated and authorized by the Issuing Bank to pay, to incur a deferred payment undertaking, to accept draft (s) or to negotiate. In a freely negotiable credit, any bank is a nominated bank.

- The Reimbursing Bank - is the bank authorized to honor the reimbursement claim in settlement of negotiation / acceptance / payment lodged with it by the paying, negotiating or accepting bank. It is normally the bank with which Issuing Bank has account, from which payment is to be made.

i)   Categories of Letter of Credit

- <u>Revocable</u>

It is an LC which can be amended or cancelled by the Issuing Bank at any time prior to its expiry without notice to the Beneficiary.

- <u>Irrevocable</u>

An irrevocable letter of credit can neither be amended nor cancelled without the agreement of all parties to the credit. LC Opening Bank gives a binding undertaking to the supplier provided all the terms and conditions of the credit are fulfilled.

- ### Unconfirmed

The Advising Bank forwards to the seller, the letter of credit, confirming its authenticity without adding its own undertaking to make payment or accept responsibility for payment.

- ### Confirmed

A confirmed letter of credit is one in which the Advising Bank adds a confirmation that payment will be made as long as compliant documents are presented. This commitment holds even if the issuing bank or the buyer fails to make payment.

- ### Standby Letters of Credit

A standby letter of credit is used as support where an alternative method of payment has been agreed. This acts like a guarantee where if the seller fails to receive payment from the buyer through the alternative method, he can claim the payment under the standby letter of credit by submitting documents stipulated in the standby LC.

- ### Revolving Letter of Credit

The revolving credit is used for regular sale of the same commodity to the same buyer. It can revolve in relation to time or value. In terms of time, it would stipulate how many times, the LC stands re-instated after first utilization; number of times the documents can be submitted within the validity period of the LC. If the credit revolves in relation to value once utilized and paid the value can be reinstated for further drawings.

- ## Transferable Letter of Credit

A transferable letter of credit is one in which the seller has the right to request the paying, or negotiating bank to make either part, or all, of the credit value available to one or more third parties. This type of credit is useful for those acting as middlemen especially where there is a need to finance purchases from third party suppliers.

- ## Back-to-Back Letter of Credit

After the letter of credit is received by the Beneficiary (seller) from the opening bank, that letter of credit is used as security by Beneficiary to establish a second letter of credit in favor of another seller from whom the Beneficiary proposes to buy the goods and send under the original LC received by him.

- ## Red clause Letter of Credit

Under this LC, the Issuing Bank authorizes the Advising/Paying Bank to make advance payment to the Beneficiary before the actual shipment of goods to the Applicant. The advance may be up to 100% of the export contract value and may be used by the Beneficiary to buy inputs for manufacturing or shipment. The Advising/Paying Bank has to ensure that the documents submitted by the Beneficiary for the goods shipment are negotiated to repay the advance made under the said Red Clause LC.

- ## Green clause Letter of Credit

It is an LC which enables the Beneficiary to receive pre-shipment advances against collateral represented by the warehouse receipt. A green clause LC differs from a red clause LC in that the goods must be warehoused. It is commonly used in the export of agricultural commodities, where the Beneficiary may raise funds to harvest new crops for export by pledging available stocks as collateral.

ii) Types of Letter of Credit

- Documentary LC (DP) – where the documents of title to the goods are required to be submitted by the Seller and the payment is to be paid immediately upon submission of the documents.

- Documentary LC (DA) – where the documents of title to the goods are required to be submitted by the Seller and the documents are delivered to the buyer immediately against acceptance but the payment is to be paid after stipulated period (like 30/60/90/120 days).

- Clean LC (DP) – documents of title to the goods are not required to be submitted under the LC and the payment is made immediately upon submission of the documents.

- Clean LC (DA) – documents of title to the goods are not required to be submitted under the LC and the other stipulated documents are delivered to the buyer immediately against acceptance but the payment is to be paid after stipulated period (like 30/60/90/120 days).

iii) Process Flow

1. Application for LC submitted by the Buyer (Applicant) to his bank (Issuing Bank)

2. Issuance of LC – Bank verifies terms and conditions of the LC and ensures that they are in conformity with terms of sanction, UCPDC 600 and other applicable guidelines. The LC is issued in favor of the beneficiary using SWIFT and advised through Advising/ Confirming Bank.

3. Advising/Confirming Bank advises LC to the Seller

4. Letter manufactures/prepares goods and ships as per LC terms.

5. Seller presents documents to the Advising/ Confirming/Paying Bank

6. Paying Bank scrutinizes documents with the LC and if found compliant, pays to the Seller and takes reimbursement from the Issuing Bank as per arrangement

7. Paying Bank sends documents to the Issuing Bank

8. Issuing Bank advises the Applicant (its customer) and recovers the amount

9. Issuing Bank sends received documents to the Applicant upon recovery of the amount/dues

FLOW CHART

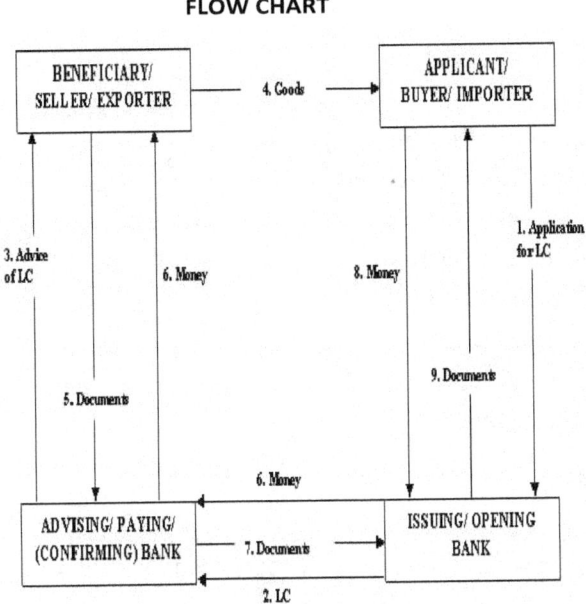

iv) **Operational Features**

- LCs are often used as a means of finance when the goods are purchased on credit (D/A LCs). The documents received under the LC are delivered against acceptance of the customer of the LC opening bank (Applicant) and the payment is made after the expiry of the credit period. The Applicant is thus able to have his working capital requirement funded through LC to the extent of value of the purchased goods for the period of credit. On due date, bank pays to the seller and recovers the amount from the customer (the Applicant).

- As stated above an LC is a tool to facilitate payment of a trade transaction. It is distinct and separate from the trade contract on which it is based. It solely deals with documents, not goods.

- The Issuing Bank's obligation to the Applicant is to ensure that the payment is released only upon strict compliance of the terms and conditions of the LC. The Applicant has irrevocable obligation to pay to the Issuing Bank notwithstanding any dispute that he might have with the Beneficiary in the matter or otherwise.

- The Paying Bank is responsible for sending the documents to the Issuing Bank to claim reimbursement.

- The most common documents include:

  - Commercial Invoice - The commercial invoice is a bill for the goods/services sold by the Beneficiary to the Applicant. It contains a description of the merchandise/service, price, point of origin, names and addresses of the Applicant (buyer), Beneficiary (seller) and shipper, and the delivery & payment terms. The Applicant needs the commercial invoice for accounting and payment of duties etc.

  - Bill of Lading - A bill of lading is the shipping document issued by the shipping company, containing details of goods and a promise to deliver the goods at the stated destination to the holder of the document in due course.

  - Certificate of Origin - This is a certificate issued by appropriate authority as required by the Applicant, attesting the place of origin of the goods. It is required in some countries as per their import and tariff regulations.

- <u>Inspection Certificate</u> - Often buyers and/or countries require it for attesting specifications of the goods. Inspection is usually performed by an independent certification organization or a representative of the buyer.

- <u>Insurance Certificate</u> - This document is issued and signed by an insurance company, agent or underwriter. It states the type and amount of coverage.

- <u>Packaging List</u> - This is itemized list of the materials in each individual package with details of net/gross weight, number of articles etc.

- <u>Warranty</u> – It is given by the seller to the buyer for the product sold.

- <u>Amendment of LC</u>

  Any request from the applicant for amendment in the LC terms and conditions is processed in a manner similar to the procedure adopted for Issuance of LC. Amendment may pertain to either increase in tenor of the LC or increase in the LC amount which should be in line with the terms of sanction. The amendment is informed to the beneficiary in a manner similar to opening of LC

- <u>Crystallizing Bills under LC</u>

  In the event of non-realization of an export bill negotiated within 30 days from the expiry of transit period (in case of sight bills) and 30 days after due date in case of usance period, the liability on the foreign currency bill is crystallized in to Indian Rupees. The foreign currency amount of the bill is converted at TT selling rate and debited to Overdue Export Bills account.

- **Expiry of LC Unutilized**

  Upon expiry of the LC if no bills are received against the LC, the LC is cancelled and the contingent liability is reversed. However, if the bills are available for negotiation with the Advising Bank, then the bank's liability remains valid even if the documents are received later. Confirmation of the Advising/Paying Bank is usually taken before cancellation of the LC.

v) Accounting Entries

- **Opening of a Letter of Credit**

1	Debit	-	Customers' liability on account of LCs opened a/c
	Credit	-	LC opened a/c (Off Balance Sheet Entry)
2	Debit	-	Customer a/c
	Credit	-	Commission (LC) a/c
	Credit	-	Postage a/c (Recovery of Commission and transmission charges)
3	Debit	-	Customer a/c
	Credit	-	Margin Money for LC Issue (Margin for LC recovered from Customer)

- **Amendment to a Letter of Credit (if increase in amount)**

1	Debit	-	Customers' liability on account of LCs opened a/c
	Credit	-	LC opened a/c (Off Balance Sheet Entry for increase in amount) Effecting amendment in the LC - increase in amount (Reverse entry in case of either reduction amount or cancellation of LC)
2	Debit	-	Customer a/c
	Credit	-	Commission (LC) a/c
	Credit	-	Postage a/c (Recovery of Commission and transmission charges for Amendment)
3	Debit	-	Customer a/c
	Credit	-	Margin Money for LC Issue (Margin for increased amount of LC recovered from Customer) (Reverse entry for reduction or cancellation)

- **Acceptance & Payment of Bills under LC**

1	Debit	-	LC opened a/c
	Credit	-	Customers' liability on account of LCs opened a/c (Off Balance Sheet Entry)

2	Debit	-	Customer's Liability for Documents Accepted under LC a/c
	Credit	-	Liability for Documents Accepted under LC a/c (Off Balance Sheet Entry for liability)

On payment, bank recovers amount payable/paid to Beneficiary together with Commission (LC bills) a/c, Postage Charges and Interest (in case of Sight LC) from the date of payment to Beneficiary to the date of payment by the Beneficiary.

- **Entries in case payment is not made on due date**

1	Debit	-	Liability for Documents Accepted under LC a/c
	Credit	-	Liability for Overdue Documents Accepted under LC a/c (Off Balance Sheet Entry for liability)
2	Debit	-	Overdue Bills a/c
	Credit	-	DD / other remittance techniques used / correspondent bank a/c (Payment to the Paying Bank which negotiated the documents)

- **When payment is made after the due date**

1	Debit	-	Customer a/c
	Credit	-	Commission (LC Bills) a/c
	Credit		Postage Charges a/c
	Credit		Overdue Bills a/c (Payment made earlier through Overdue Bill a/c reversed)

2	Debit	-	Liability for Overdue Documents Accepted under LC a/ Customer's Liability for Documents
	Credit	-	Accepted under LC a/c (Off Balance Sheet Entry for liability)
	Credit	-	Interest on Bills (LC) a/c

(Recovery of Commission on LC Bills, Postage Charges and interest from the date of payment of amount to negotiating bank till date of recovery from the customer, including penal interest)

vi) Benefits of Letter of Credit

- The beneficiary is assured of payment as long as it complies with the terms and conditions of the letter of credit. The credit risk is transferred from the applicant to the issuing bank.

- The beneficiary is able to avoid country risk by seeking confirmation from a bank in his own country.

- The Applicant is able to buy the goods as per his specifications, duly inspected/certified by his agent in seller's country and dispatch through goods carriers of his choice.

- The Applicant is able get credit from the seller based on credit worthiness of his bank.

vii) Risks in Letter of Credit

- Since all the parties involved in Letter of Credit deal with the documents and not with the goods, the risk of Beneficiary not shipping goods as mentioned in the LC is still remains though Applicant seeks to overcome this by getting the goods inspected by his local agent/ representative.

- The Letter of Credit as a payment method is costlier than other methods of payment

- The Beneficiary's documents must strictly comply with the terms and conditions of the Letter of Credit for Issuing Bank to make the payment. The documents are exposed to the risk of rejection if any discrepancy is found in documents.

II.   BILLS NEGOTIATION UNDER LC

a.   Negotiation of Bills

Negotiation refers to giving value for documents and / or drafts by the bank authorized to negotiate under credit. The negotiating bank is required to pay the seller on submission of the necessary documents, as detailed in the LC. Documents tendered under the LC must be in conformity with the terms and conditions contained in the LC. Any irregularity in the documents vis-a-vis the clauses incorporated in the LC or documents which appear inconsistent will absolve the issuing bank of its liability to honor the drawings. It is thus necessary for a thorough scrutiny of the documents presented under the LC. In case of discrepancies in the documents submitted to the negotiating bank, the negotiating bank may choose to negotiate the discrepant documents under reserve. Negotiation under reserve is undertaken after obtaining a letter of indemnity from the exporter to indemnify the negotiating bank in case the discrepant documents are returned by the issuing bank.

The negotiation of the documents under LC may not be restricted to a particular bank. In that event, any bank may choose to negotiate the documents as mutually agreed to between it and the Beneficiary. There is no obligation for the bank to negotiate the documents unless so stated by it.

b. Advising of Export Letters of Credit

The LC issued by the Issuing Bank is advised to the Beneficiary by a Bank. The Advising Bank's role is authentication of the LC.

Bank receives LCs for advising from overseas correspondents as well as non-correspondent banks. All LCs are to be advised to the beneficiaries after checking the apparent authenticity of the LC and ensuring compliance with respect to prevailing regulations including UCPDC, Exchange Control and Trade Policy of the country.

Issuing Bank may precede the LC with a brief pre-advice which contains the words 'Full Details to Follow'. The pre-advice is not the operative credit and only contains the brief summary of the transaction.

c. Adding Confirmation to Letters of Credit

The Issuing Bank may have the LC confirmed to the Beneficiary by a bank. In that case, the Confirming Bank takes upon itself the responsibility to negotiate the documents as per LC terms. Confirmation is an extension of advising of credit. The bank not only advises the LC but adds its guarantee to the undertaking given by the Issuing Bank. It is an undertaking on part of the confirming bank, in addition to that of the Issuing Bank, provided the documents are presented to the confirming bank and that the terms and conditions of the credit are complied with. Hence, adding of confirmation entails assessment of risk on the Issuing Bank and the country of the Issuing Bank. Since the Confirming Bank is present at the Seller's location, the Seller gets the comfort of assurance from a local bank.

At the request of the Issuing Bank, confirmation can be added by the Advising bank to the LC. Confirmation can also be added to the LC at the request of the Beneficiary but after obtaining the consent of the Issuing Bank.

After the bank has added confirmation, the credit may be amended by the Issuing Bank. In such cases amendments would be sent to the confirming bank for advising them to the beneficiary. If the confirming bank passes on the amendments to the Beneficiary, it amounts to the confirming bank's concurrence for such amendment and consequently its confirmation extends to such amendment.

d. Accounting Entries

LC Advising

Debit	-	Customer a/c
Credit	-	Commission (LC) a/c
Credit	-	Postage charges a/c

Advising Amendment to LC

Debit	-	Customer a/c
Credit	-	Commission (LC) a/c
Credit	-	Postage Charges a/c

Confirming a LC

Debit	Liability on account of LC Confirmation a/c
Credit	Issuing Bank's liability on account of LC Confirmation a/c (Off Balance Sheet Entry)
Debit	Customer a/c
Credit	Commission (LC) a/c
Credit	Postage charges a/c (Charges for Confirmation of LC)

Amendment of LC

- In case of increase in the LC amount then the same entry to be passed as for the original LC confirmation, for the incremental amount and for charges.

- In case of decrease in the LC amount or cancellation of LC then the liability reversal entries to be passed.

- In case of any other amendment then only LC advising charges to be recovered i.e.

Debit - Customer a/c
Credit- Commission (LC) account
    - Credit Postage charges a/c

Expiry of confirmed unutilized LC

Debit - Issuing bank's liability on account of LC confirmation a/c
Credit - Liability on account of LC confirmation a/c

<u>Negotiation of Bill under LC</u>

Debit -   Bills Negotiated Account
Credit -   Interest (Bills under LC) a/c
Credit -   Commission (Negotiation under LC) a/c
Credit -   Postage charges a/c
Credit -   Customers current a/c

<u>On payment by Issuing Bank on due date of the bill</u>

Debit -   Correspondent Bank a/c
Credit -   Bills Negotiated Account
Credit -   Interest (Negotiation under LC) a/c

III.   BILLS PURCHASE/BILLS DISCOUNTING

As explained in Section on Bills Purchase/Discounting in Chapter on Business Banking – Assets, customers are extended facility of financing their trade bills pending their payment by the buyer. The payment terms may be sight (immediately on presentation) or usance (credit for a specified period). A documentary bill for purchase/ discounting, inter-alia, includes:

- Bill of Exchange
- Invoice
- Goods Transport Receipt/Bill of Lading

a.   Bill of Exchange

The Bill of Exchange is an instrument in writing containing an unconditional order, signed by the maker directing a certain person to pay a certain sum of money only to or the order of a certain person.

The essential requisites of a bill of exchange are:

- It should be in writing

- It must contain an order to pay

-The order contained should be unconditional

- The bill must be signed by the drawer

Parties to a Bill of Exchange

The three essential parties to a bill are:

- Drawer (seller of the goods)
- Drawee (Buyer of the goods)
- Payee (the person to whom the amount of the bill is payable)

Types of Bills of Exchange

There are two types of bills:

- **Demand bill** is a bill of exchange which is payable on demand. Sometimes a bill may contain words like payable at sight or on presentation. Such bills are also demand bills. In this case the drawee is not given any additional time, besides the transit period, to pay the bill. It does not attract stamp duty.

- **Usance bills** are drawn wherever the drawer of the bill allows credit to the drawee to settle the transaction (to make the payment). It is one which is payable on the expiry of a certain period. A usance bill is also referred to as a time bill. The drawee, in this transaction is allowed credit to settle the transaction. It attracts stamp duty, as applicable. The drawee accepts the bill on the face of it and receives other documents. On due date, he pays the bill and the accepted bill is handed over to him. In case of non-payment, the accepted bill of exchange forms an essential part of the legal documents for recovery of the dues from the drawee.

<u>Maturity of a Usance Bill</u>

There are two types of usance bills –

— bills which are payable a certain number of days/ months after sight
— bills which are payable a certain number of days/ months after date of the bill

After sight means after presentation of the bill to the drawee

In case of bills drawn in months, the period of usance will terminate on the corresponding day of the month. If the month does not have the corresponding day, the usance period terminates on the last day of the month.

If date of maturity falls on a holiday then the bill falls due for payment on the subsequent working day.

<u>Presentation of Bill for Acceptance</u>

If the bill of exchange is payable on demand, it is not necessary for the bank to present it to the drawee for acceptance. If the bill is a usance bill, the bank has to present it for acceptance. The bill should be presented by the bank without any delay after the receipt of the bill from the drawer / remitting bank. The acceptance of the bill constitutes definite commitment on part of the drawee to pay the bill on due date.

<u>Dishonor of Bills</u>

A bill may be dishonored in one of the following ways:

- Demand bill remains unpaid

- Usance bill is not accepted
- Accepted usance bill is not paid on due date

Where a bill has been dishonored by the drawee by non-acceptance or non-payment, the holder can proceed against the drawer in court after giving them due notice of dishonor. For this purpose, the bill has to be noted, which is a convenient method of authenticating the fact of dishonor.

To summarize, the various stages in the discounting of bills are:

- Receipt of documents for discounting from the drawer and scrutiny for adequate credit limit and completeness of documents.

- Approval of the transaction and credit the net amount to the drawer's account. Forward documents to the collecting bank for collecting the bill amount from the drawee.

- On realization of funds through the collecting bank, reverse the entry created for bills discounted.

- In case of dishonor and return of the bill, recover the amount from the drawer along with penal interest for the entire duration of the bill discounted period. If required, then ensure that the bill has been protested by the notary. The documents to be returned to the drawer after recovery of complete amount due to the bank.

Accounting Entries

At the time of purchase/discounting of bill

Debit   -   Bills Discounted / Purchased account

Credit   -   Interest (BP/BD) account

Credit   -   Commission (BP/BD) account

Credit   -   Postage charges account

Credit   -   Client's current account

At the time of dishonor of discounted

Debit   -   Client's current account

Credit   -   Bills Discounted /Purchased account

Credit   -   Overdue Interest (Bills) account

b. Invoice

Invoice is the Sales Bill raised by the seller on the buyer containing details of the items supplied, quantity, price and total value etc. It is the basic document for accounting of sales by the seller and the purchase by the buyer. It also records sales tax, duties etc., charged on the items. It is signed by the seller.

c. Goods Transport Receipt/Bill of Lading

When the goods are sent by the seller to the buyer by road transport or railways or through ship or though air, these transporters issue receipt containing details of consignor (sender), consignee (receiver), description of goods, quantity, location from & to and freight paid/payable. This receipt is required to be presented by the consignee to the transporter at the destination for taking delivery of the goods. This receipt is also known as document of title to the goods.

IV.   BILLS COLLECTION

A bill sent outward for collection is a bill of exchange / draft drawn payable on demand or a certain number of days after sight and lodged for collection with the bank. The proceeds of such instruments are credited / remitted to the drawer after realization of the same.

When the customer either does not have financing facility for purchase/discounting of the bill or the bill exceeds the financing limit or the bill under LC is discrepant and hence cannot be negotiated or when the seller does not need financing against the bill, the bill is sent under collection.

The seller submits bill to his bank. The bank sends the bill to the bank of the Drawee or any other bank (as per arrangement between the buyer and the seller) for presenting the same to the Drawer. The presenting bank is advised to deliver the documents against payment or acceptance as per instructions of the seller. The presenting bank collects the payment on delivery or on due date (as applicable) and remits the amount to the collecting bank. The collecting bank credits seller's account with the proceeds. The presenting and collecting banks recover their commission and charges either from the proceeds of the bill or from the buyer as per instructions of the seller.

The responsibility of the collecting bank is to the extent of following seller's instructions and act with due diligence. The presenting bank has to follow collecting bank's instructions. Any deviation in the terms requires seller's instructions.

The bill is Outward Bill for Collection in the books of customer's bank; whereas it is Inward Bill for Collection in the books of bank to which it has been sent (Presenting Bank).

Stages in the Outward Collection Process

- <u>Receipt of Documents</u>

  On receipt of documents from the drawer, it is the responsibility of the bank to strictly follow the detail of the instructions from the drawer with respect to the drawee, maturity, amount, delivery of documents, collection charges and protest.

- <u>Forwarding Documents to Issuing Bank (in case bill collection under LC) /Presenting Bank</u>

  Documents are to be forwarded to the Issuing Bank (in case bill collection under LC) /Presenting Bank. The Presenting Bank is advised in the covering schedule about the mode of remittance of realization proceeds –

  - In case it is being presented by collecting bank's own branch - direct credit to collection account of the Collecting Branch

  - In case it is to another bank in India – to remit by DD or RTGS

  - In case it is to another country – to remit by direct credit to Nostro account or authority to debit the presenting bank's Vostro or by SWIFT through credit of either collecting bank's account abroad or presenting bank's account in India other similar means of transferring credit should be stated in the forwarding letter.

Accounting entries

At the time of sending bill for collection

In Collecting Bank's books

Debit - Customer's Liability for Outward Bill
for Collection

Credit - Liability for Outward Bill for Collection

In Presenting Bank's books - on receipt of bill

Debit - Customer's Liability for Inward Bill for
Collection Account

Credit - Liability for Inward Bill for Collection
Account

At the time of payment of the bill

In Presenting Bank's books

> Debit - Customer's Account
> Credit- Other Branch/DD/RTGS/Nostro/Vostro
> Credit- Commission Account
> (Bill amount plus bank's fee)

> Debit- Liability for Inward Bill for Collection
> Account
> Credit- Customer's Liability for Inward Bill for
> Collection Account
> (Reversal of Liability)

At the time of crediting customer upon receiving amount from Presenting Bank

In Collecting Bank's books

> Debit- Clearing/Nostro/Vostro

Credit- Customer's Account

Credit- Charges Account

➢ Debit- Liability for Outward Bill for Collection

Credit - Customer's Liability for Outward Bill for Collection

V. PACKING CREDIT

Packing Credit is the pre-shipment working capital finance extended to an exporter to assist in exporting the underlying goods. Basic purpose of extending pre-shipment finance is to enable the eligible exporters to procure raw materials / process / manufacture / warehouse / ship the goods meant for exports.

PCL is defined as a loan or advance granted or any other credit provided by an institution to an exporter for financing purchase of raw materials, processing and packing of the goods, on the strength of letters of credit (LC) or a confirmed and irrevocable order or any other evidence of an order for export from India.

Packing Credit finance is given in Indian Rupee (INR) as well as in foreign currency.

Eligibility for PCL

PCL can be granted to an exporter who has an export order or LC in his own name and who will actually export the goods. However, as an exception to this rule, PCL can be granted to supporting manufacturers or suppliers of goods, who do not have export order or LC in their own name and who are exporting through export houses. In these cases, the eligible PCL amount can be shared between the two parties involved.

Criteria for Granting PCL

It is granted to eligible exporters against lodgment of irrevocable LC (established through reputed bank) or confirmed order placed by overseas buyers for export of goods from India.

Bank can also extend PCL against messages exchanged between the buyer and exporter provided such messages contain the following information:

(1) Name of the overseas buyer (2) Particulars of goods to be exported (3) Quantity and unit prices or value of order (4) Date of shipment (5) Terms of sales and payment

Bank must follow-up in these cases to obtain the final contract / LC within a reasonable period.

Running Account Facilities

Bank is also authorized to grant pre-shipment advances for exports without insisting on prior lodgment of LC / firm export order. However, the need of the exporter for this facility has to be established by the bank and restricted to the exporters with good track record. Further, the LC / firm export order needs to be produced by the exporter within a reasonable period of time.

Purpose of Finance

PCL is granted for the specific purpose of procuring raw material / purchasing / manufacturing / transporting / Warehousing / packing and shipping the goods.

Form of Finance

PCL is usually a funded advance. Bank, has to be ensured that there is no double financing against a particular export order.

Quantum of Finance

There is no fixed formula for determining the quantum of finance to be granted to an exporter against a specific order / LC or an expected order. However, the quantum should be need based, depending on nature of order, commodity, and capability of exporter. Accordingly, the percentage of margin is determined. The PCL granted does not normally exceed the CIF value of goods or domestic market value of the goods.

Period of Finance

PCL is basically a short-term finance (90/180/270 days). Maximum period for which PCL can be granted at concessional rates is determined by RBI. Extensions in the period of financing are permitted subject to RBI approvals.

Rate of Interest

It is obligatory on the parts of the banks to charge interest on PCL as per the interest stipulated by RBI at a particular point of time. If exports are not undertaken within a reasonable period of time then the benefit of concessional interest rate is removed and higher interest rates are applicable from the first day of the advance.

Interest is to be recovered quarterly from the PCL advances by debit to the respective customer current account.

Maintenance of Accounts

Banks are required to segregate and maintain separately the accounts in respect to which each PCL advance is disbursed. Running Account Facility is the only exception to this.

Follow-Up & Monitoring

Banks extending PCL are required to follow-up and monitor the accounts to ensure that the ultimate objective is achieved.

Liquidation of PCL

PCL advance must be repaid by the exporter through the proceeds of export bills negotiated, purchased or discounted. If export of goods does not take place within the stipulated period and/or the PCL amount is repaid out of other than export proceeds, then bank have to charge normal interest rate as applicable for domestic business.

PCL should not remain outstanding once the relative goods are exported and documents are tendered to the bank.

Accounting entries –

Disbursal of PCL

Debit -	Packing credit (Rupees) a/c
Credit -	Customer current a/c

Recovery of Interest*

Debit -	Customer current account
Credit -	P/L Interest on Packing

Recovery of ECGC Premium*

Debit - Customer current account

Credit - Suspense A/c ECGC Prem. on Packing Credit

*recovered monthly

Liquidation of PCL loan a/c

(on submission of Export Documents)

Debit - Foreign Bills Purchased/Foreign Bills Discounting/Foreign Bills Negotiated

Credit - Packing Credit (Rupees) account

VI. GUARANTEE

Banks issue guarantees on behalf of their customers for various purposes. While guarantees may be required by individuals for their personal needs, most of the time, bank guarantees are required for business needs. These guarantees may be required to secure advance payment received by the customer, for retiring goods from transporter or shipping company without producing goods receipt/bill of lading/air consignment note, for participating in bidding process without making cash payment of the earnest money, for assuring performance of the equipment supplied by the customer etc.

The bank guarantee is an irrevocable commitment by the bank to make a payment to the beneficiary specified in the bank guarantee on demand. It is issued on behalf of bank's customer in favor of a client of the bank's customer. It is always unconditional promise to pay the amount on demand irrespective of any dispute between the bank's customer and its client with regard to justification for raising the demand. The demand from the client under the guarantee within its validity period is all that is required of the client to claim payment of the amount from the bank. It is entirely between customer and its client to settle their differences outside the domain of the guarantee or go to the court; but the guarantee once invoked by the client, has to be paid immediately.

Key features of a bank guarantee are:

- It is only for payment of specified amount in the guarantee.

- It has a certain specific expiry date and a claim period within which the beneficiary can lodge the claim. Beneficiary cannot claim any amount after that date.

- The guarantee though refers to the contract between the customer of the bank and the beneficiary, the payment obligation of the bank is totally unqualified;

- Customer cannot ask the Bank to hold back the invoked claim under any circumstances. If, however bank receives court order not to be pay, only then bank can withhold the payment.

- Bank to pay the amount even if it is unable to recover from its customer.

  As stated above, Bank issues guarantees on behalf of its customers in favor of their clients for various purposes like:

  - To secure advance paid to bank's customer by a client for supply of goods/services.

- To submit bid, customer may submit guarantee in lieu of required earnest money.

- To enable the customer to take delivery of the goods from transport company/shipping company/airlines without submitting transport receipt/bill of lading/air consignment note.

- To assure buyer of plant/equipment of its performance on behalf of bank's customer.

- To secure payment of the cost of plant/machinery in installments in future to the supplier by bank's customer

Depending on the purpose, guarantees are classified as:

a. Financial Guarantee

To substitute money are financial guarantees. For example:

- Advance Payment Guarantee to secure advance received by the customer
- Bid Bond (in lieu of Earnest Money)
- Deferred Payment Guarantee

b. Performance Guarantee

To assure performance of its products, bank's customer may provide bank guarantee to his buyer. In case of unsatisfactory performance, the buyer may invoke the guarantee and demand payment of money specified under the guarantee.

Banks may or may not take security (cash or otherwise) for issuing the guarantees. Accordingly, the guarantees are categorized as "Clean" of "Secured" Guarantees.

RBI has issued guidelines to the banks for issuing guarantees, key points whereof are given below:

- Banks should normally issue financial guarantees. They should exercise due caution with regard to performance guarantee business.

- Banks are discouraged to issue guarantees for longer period.

- Bank guarantee should not normally be valid for more than 10 years.

- Banks should avoid issuing unsecured guarantees in large amounts and for medium and long-term periods.

- Banks should avoid undue concentration of such unsecured guarantee commitments to particular groups of customers and/or trades.

- Banks should exercise extra caution while issuing unsecured guarantees or guarantees for deferred payment.

c. Shipping Guarantee

Shipping Guarantees are very common among importers due to the advancement of transport system and cargo handling procedures. As a result, vessel reach their intended destinations before documents reach the importer. In such circumstances, importers are anxious to clear the goods to avoid –

– paying demurrage

- in case of seasonal imports, delay in clearance will reduce the marketability of the imported goods
- possible damages to perishable and sensible goods
- production losses due to delay in receipt of goods

In the event of goods reaching the destination before the receipt of original documents by the buyer the original B/L is not available to the buyer to clear the goods. In such circumstances shipping agent may release cargo in the absence of original B/L provided they are indemnified against all consequence that may follow as a result of delivering goods without surrendering the original B/L. By issuing shipping guarantee, bank takes up the entire risk upon itself by agreeing to compensate the shipping line.

The Shipping Guarantee enables the customer to take delivery of the goods before the receipt of the bill of lading. It is an indemnity that the bank executes jointly and severally with its customers in favor of the shipping company. For shipment by air, the bank would be asked to endorse the airway bill to the order of the customer to take the goods. A Shipping Guarantee or airway bill endorsement is issued by banks for a customer having regular trading facilities. Otherwise, banks issue this guarantee against 100% margin.

Some of the special terms in Shipping Guarantee are:

- It is to be issued in a format acceptable to the shipping company (in the format issued by them)
- Cover may be up to 150 to 300 pct of the invoice of the goods.
- It is open ended (There is no expiry for shipping guarantee)

— Claim need not be supported by any other document. Payable simply on demand.

The guarantee continues until the original bill of lading is surrendered or the cancelled guarantee is received back. Therefore, banks have to exercise extra care while issuing the guarantee. Banks usually issue these guarantees only where they have issued the LC to ensure that the documents containing original bill of lading is routed through them. In other cases, they usually take 100% or more cash margin. The details of the invoice are scrutinized with the goods under bill of lading to ensure that they strictly match.

<u>Accounting Entries</u>

Issuing a Bank Guarantee does not create any financial transaction. The financial transaction at that time is only in respect of taking margin and commission. Following entries are passed by the bank at the time of issuing the guarantee.

➢ Debit - Customer's Liability for Guarantee Issue

Credit - Bank's Liability for Guarantee Issue (Off Balance Sheet – Liability created)

➢ Debit - Customer's Account

Credit - Margin Money for Guarantee

Credit - Profit & Loss Commission on Guarantee (Margin plus Commission recovery from the customer)

The financial transaction occurs if and when the guarantee is invoked and paid to the beneficiary. Following entries are passed at the time of payment:

- ➤ Debit -   Customer's Account
  Debit -   Margin Money for Guarantee
  Credit - Demand Draft/Pay Order Issue
  (Payment amount recovered from customer's account and Margin account)

- ➤ Debit -   Bank's Liability for Guarantee Issue

  Credit - Customer's Liability for Guarantee Issue (Off Balance Sheet – Liability reversed)

If the guarantee is not invoked and expires, after expiry of the claim period, following entries are passed at the time of expiry of the guarantee and claim period:

- ➤ Debit -   Bank's Liability for Guarantee Issue
  Credit - Customer's Liability for Guarantee Issue (Off Balance Sheet – Liability reversed)

- ➤ Debit -   Margin Money for Guarantee
  Credit - Customer's Account
  (Margin amount repaid to the customer)

VII.   INCOTERMS

Incoterms or International Commercial terms are a series of international sales terms, published by International Chamber of Commerce (ICC) and widely used in international commercial transactions. These are accepted by governments, legal authorities and practitioners worldwide for the interpretation of most commonly used terms in international trade. This reduces or removes altogether uncertainties arising from different interpretation of such terms in different countries. Scope of this is limited to matters relating to rights and obligations of the parties to the contract of sale with respect to the delivery of goods sold. They are used to divide transaction costs and responsibilities between buyer and seller and reflect state-of-the-art transportation practices. They closely correspond to the U.N. Convention on Contracts for the International Sale of Goods. The first version was introduced in 1936. As of January 1, 2011, the eighth edition, Incoterms 2010 is in effect.

Summary of terms

Group C – Main carriage paid

- **CFR or CNF** – Cost and Freight (named destination port)

  Seller must pay the costs and freight to bring the goods to the port of destination. However, risk is transferred to the buyer once the goods have crossed the ship's rail. Maritime transport only and Insurance for the goods is NOT included. Insurance is at the Cost of the Buyer.

- **CIF** – Cost, Insurance and Freight (named destination port)
  Exactly the same as CFR except that the seller must in addition procure and pay for insurance for the buyer Maritime transport only.

- **CPT** – Carriage Paid To (named place of destination)

The general/containerized/multimodal equivalent of CFR. The seller pays for carriage to the named point of destination, but risk passes when the goods are handed over to the first carrier.

- **CIP** – Carriage and Insurance Paid (To) (named place of destination)

The containerized transport/multimodal equivalent of CIF. Seller pays for carriage and insurance to the named destination point, but risk passes when the goods are handed over to the first carrier.

Group D – Arrival

- **DAF** – Delivered At Frontier

This term can be used when the goods are transported by rail and road. The seller pays for transportation to the named place of delivery at the frontier. The buyer arranges for customs clearance and pays for transportation from the frontier to his factory. The passing of risk occurs at the frontier.

- **DES** – Delivered Ex Ship (named port)

Where goods are delivered ex ship, the passing of risk does not occur until the ship has arrived at the named port of destination and the goods made available for unloading to the buyer. The seller pays the same freight and insurance costs as he would under a CIF arrangement. Unlike CFR and CIF terms, the seller has agreed to bear not just cost, but also Risk and Title up to the arrival of the vessel at the named port. Costs for unloading the goods and any duties, taxes, etc.... are for the Buyer.

- **DEQ** – Delivered Ex Quay (named port)

  This is similar to DES, but the passing of risk does not occur until the goods have been unloaded at the port of destination.

- **DDU** – Delivered Duty Unpaid (named destination place)

  This term means that the seller delivers the goods to the buyer to the named place of destination in the contract of sale. The goods are not cleared for import or unloaded from any form of transport at the place of destination. The buyer is responsible for the costs and risks for the unloading, duty and any subsequent delivery beyond the place of destination. However, if the buyer wishes the seller to bear cost and risks associated with the import clearance, duty, unloading and subsequent delivery beyond the place of destination, then this all needs to be explicitly agreed upon in the contract of sale.

- **DDP** – Delivered Duty Paid (named destination place)

  This term means that the seller pays for all transportation costs and bears all risk until the goods have been delivered and pays the duty. Also used interchangeably with the term "Free Domicile". The most comprehensive term for the buyer. In most of the importing countries, taxes such as (but not limited to) VAT and excises should not be considered prepaid being handled as a "refundable" tax. Therefore, VAT and excises usually are not representing a direct cost for the importer since they will be recovered against the sales on the local (domestic) market.

Group E – Departure

- **EXW** – Ex Works (named place)

  The seller makes the goods available at his premises. The buyer is responsible for all charges.

Group F – Main carriage unpaid

- **FCA** – Free Carrier (named places)

  The seller hands over the goods, cleared for export, into the custody of the first carrier (named by the buyer) at the named place. This term is suitable for all modes of transport, including carriage by air, rail, road, and containerized / multi-modal sea transport. This is the correct "freight collect" term to use for sea shipments in containers, whether LCL (less than container load) or FCL (full container load).

- **FAS** – Free Alongside Ship (named loading port)

  The seller must place the goods alongside the ship at the named port. The seller must clear the goods for export. Suitable only for maritime transport only but NOT for multimodal sea transport in containers (see Incoterms 2010, ICC publication 715). This term is typically used for heavy-lift or bulk cargo.

- **FOB** – Free on Board (named loading port)

  The seller must himself load the goods on board the ship nominated by the buyer, cost and risk being divided at ship's rail. The seller must clear the goods for export. Maritime transport only but NOT for multimodal sea transport in containers. The buyer must instruct the seller the details of the vessel and port where the goods are to be loaded, and there is no reference to, or provision for, the use of a carrier or forwarder. It DOES NOT include Air transport.

CHAPTER 3
CASH MANAGEMENT SERVICES

I. INTRODUCTION

Cash Management Services (CMS), in the present context, means managing cash inflows and outflows of an organization. In simple terms it means managing the payables & receivables. A big company would normally have a very large number of suppliers, clients, employees and shareholders spread over nook and corner of the country. Each one is a source of cash inflow or outflow. Some of them may be easily connected while many others may be in remote areas where it takes time to connect. To manage cash inflows/outflows from all of them efficiently is a challenge. Companies face a number of issues like slow movement of funds, locked working capital, loss of float income, high cost of funds and reconciliation etc. Efficiency in terms of time and cost contributes in improving liquidity and profitability. Companies look for solutions which save time, processing cost, administrative cost, reconciliation effort, on-line information and MIS to track & control outstandings. Banks have evolved various technology driven Cash Management Service products to provide the solutions for each of these issues.

Cash Management in India

Traditionally the transactions have been paper-based which involved manual handling which was time consuming, riskier and costlier. Electronic banking, which began as a passive desktop access to bank balances, is emerging into complex processes of liquidity management through numerous techniques. The adoption of electronic medium has opened up a vast opportunity to do away with the paper. Of late, the electronic payment systems introduced in the banking system like NEFT, RTGS, NACH, Cheque Truncation (Image processing), anywhere banking through Core Banking Solution, Internet Banking and MICR processing have resulted in paradigm shift. In such an environment, the ability to recognize and capture market share depends entirely on the bank's competence to evolve technically and offer the customer a seamless process flow.

The Reserve Bank of India (RBI) has placed an emphasis on upgrading technological infrastructure. Electronic Banking, Cheque Imaging, Enterprise Resource Planning (ERP) and Real Time Gross Settlement (RTGS) are just few of the new initiatives. For example, the Enactment of Information Technology Act gives legal recognition to electronic records and digital signatures.

The Cash Management can be broadly categorized in to Collection and Payment. Banks are in normal course engaged in doing these activities for all their customers. The basic difference in CMS is that it takes over entire activity of big companies in regard to collection and payment in such a way that it reduces their pressure to handle large volumes quickly, provides those details which in normal banking are not provided by banks and provides customized MIS solutions to reduce effort in reconciliation and tracking realizations. Over and above this, it takes over customer's work of writing cheque, issuing/delivering warrants, picking up cheques from clients etc.

Banks incur cost and time on this because this helps them in getting remunerative account of big companies which provides them free float as well as fee on services provided for the activity. In the competitive environment of today, CMS is an essential product for any bank to attract large company's account.

For providing these services there are primarily 4 following enablers:

- Network of bank's own branches and of their correspondent banks which enables collection of upcountry cheques from various locations and delivery of payment instruments quickly

- Core Banking Solution (CBS) which helps in providing anywhere banking, validation and control on large number of collections and payments

- Electronic Payment System enabled by RBI – helps in providing safe and quick debits & credits between various banks

- CMS software having on-line link to CBS which (1) handles volumes of collections and payments (2) provides customized detailed MIS to customers (3) controls and tracks printing and dispatch of payment instruments

II. PROCESS

- CMS Software of the bank handles all front-end activities while the CBS is used to record consolidated entries in the customer account. The interface between CMS software and the CBS is mostly on "batch processing" basis which generates transaction entries.

- For example, the cheques received for clearing are lodged in CMS software and the batch processing creates single entry in the Clearing Module for each CMS customer for the aggregate amount. Similarly, for clearing cheque returns, the system debits CMS Clearing Account from where the CMS software does the internal processing of individual entries.

- Similarly, for outstation cheques collection, the entries are done in CMS software which generates covering schedules.

- The transactions through Internet Banking are also uploaded in CMS software, either through "Straight Through Processing" or through file upload depending upon technology structure at each bank.

- For payments, likewise, the details are generated by the CMS software to be fed into CBS in the required format for onward transmission.

- CMS data is customized for each customer to include required information. For example, for a deposit of cheque, the data may contain cheque number, name of the drawer of the cheque, bank and branch name, date of cheque and amount in addition to bank's customer account details. Banks even provide scanned copies of instruments, if so required by the customer; which again is a function which is linked to CMS software.

- In short, every entry first moves into CMS software, gets processed there and the accounting entry is batch uploaded into CBS while other processing and MIS etc., are taken care of in CMS software.

- CMS Software is practically a part of online banking except for the banks where CMS software talks to CBS on batch processing basis.

- With the help of standardized messaging system now in vogue in most of the software packages, the flow of information and transaction between different software is straight through, online. The customer is therefore able to access information processed in various software solutions in an integrated manner through internet and phone banking.

III. COLLECTION

The collection service offered by banks has following distinct features:

- Faster processing of collections with timely intimation
- Collection across multiple locations through branches and correspondents
- Receivables process
- Processing of cheques in bulk and direct debit mandates
- Instant credit facility on mutually agreed terms
- Takeover of Receivables and Reconciliation
- Web based information

Item-wise process for collection is described in the following paragraphs:

a. **Cheques**

- Cheques drawn on own branch locations of the bank
- Cheques drawn on correspondent bank's branch locations
- Cheques drawn on locations not having branch or its correspondent banks
- Postdated cheque collections
- Local as well as outstation cheque collections
- Pooling of funds into one single account
- Collection of funds in customized accounts' structure
- Fixed date confirmed credit as per mutual arrangement
- Client level customized MIS reports –
  - Deposit slip-wise query with instrument drill down
  - Instrument-wise query
  - Reports scheduling
  - Reports on demand
  - Delivery status of scheduled reports
  - Location wise/date wise, monthly cumulative, monthly charges statement, monthly cheque return statement
  - ERP compliant
  - Cheque pick-up from customers door step
  - Option to forward data in soft copy form in a secure environment
  - Credit Forecast report
  - Single collection account for cheque deposits across the country
  - Cash concentration in the centralized collection account

- Collection reports with details of cheque number, drawer's name, date and place of deposit and invoice details
- Online querying on instruments deposited across the country
- One platform for all forms of collections i.e., cheques, cash and electronic Automated Bank
- Automated Reconciliation through integration of collection reports with Back Office Systems
- Reconciliation of invoices against receipts from customers

b. **NACH - Debit**

- NACH (Debit) is normally used for collections which include payment of utility bills (electricity, telephone), collection of taxes etc.

- NACH (Debit) facility can be availed at locations listed for the purpose (having CBS platform)

- Following broad steps are required to be taken:

- The company needs to obtain a mandate from the beneficiary / payee which would provide all the details as stipulated by Reserve Bank of India.

- The Company will have to route the transaction through a Sponsor Bank.

- The Company is required to submit an E1 form to get a User code from RBI through the Sponsor Bank. One user code is obtained for NACH at all RBI locations.

- The data has to be provided to the Sponsor Bank preferably 7 working days before the settlement date (on which the account of the beneficiary will be debited).

- B-NACH facility is also used for catering the business requirements of the corporate to handle the hefty volume in bulk manner. At present, the requisite data of the mandate in B-NACH is uploaded in Excel Sheet.

- Now a day, in technology era, E-NACH facility is also provided to the customers in order to register their mandate electronically instead of physical form through Net Banking facility and Debit/Credit Card credentials.

c. **Receivables Management System**

- Consolidate receivables information across electronic and paper collections

- Automate accounts receivables reconciliation using pre-defined matching parameters for funds received against various invoices

- Deliver collection reports structured to meet specified needs

- Provide online transaction enquiry

Benefits of CMS to Customers

- Confirmed arrangements

- Outsourced logistics

- Enhanced clearing network

- Pooling / Single Payout Account

- Eliminating idle cash balances monitoring exposure and reducing risks.

- Ensuring timely deposit of collections

- Assured payment on fixed day basis, irrespective of the fate of the instrument sent in for clearing

- Instrument outstanding report and credits in the pipeline report available to strengthen internal control

- Multiple channels available for receipt of data including e-mails, faxes, courier and the Internet

- Availability of scan images of instruments at select locations

IV. PAYMENT

The collection service offered by banks has following distinct features:

- Integrated Receivable and Payable System

- Takeover of entire Payables management of the client including tracking of Payments

- Multiple modes of Payments viz., cheques, demand drafts, RTGS, NEFT, SWIFT etc.

- Web based information to the client

- Faster Straight Through Processing

Companies have to make payments to several entities - vendor payments, mass payments of dividend and interest, taxes etc. CMS offers cost effective way of low-value, high volume payments through -

a. Demand Drafts/Bankers' Cheques

Banks provide facility of issuing in bulk Demand Drafts/Banker's Cheques as per customer's requirements and deliver the same to the beneficiaries directly under advice. The data is received from the customer in soft copy either on mail or through Internet upload. The data is downloaded and printed centrally or at the payees' locations. The instruments are sent to the beneficiaries by the local branches/CMS centers as per customer's requirement. The customer is provided with the MIS about the issued instruments, paid/unpaid etc., as required by the customer.

b. Internet-Based Cheque Writing

Banks provide printing facility at customer's premises, based on information provided in soft form or directly uploaded through Internet Banking; thus eliminating time involved in delivery of the cheques.

Following features are offered in this:

- Along with printing the instrument, the customer has an option to print the cover note advice and imprint the facsimile signature of the signatories of the company. The advice shows beneficiary details and some additional fields of information as required.

- Web-based access for uploading and authorizing printing requests

- ERP/CRM extractor for extracting data directly from the ERP/CRM system

- Host-To-Host connectivity for Straight Through Processing of transactions

- Data encryption for enhanced security

- Partial batch authorization and processing

- Dynamic signature printing

- Printing of instruments and direct dispatch to beneficiaries

- Tracking of dispatches

- Advices over e-mail to beneficiaries

- Online querying & reconciliation of instruments through varied reports

- Outsourcing of instrument dispatches directly to the beneficiaries

- Remote authorization of payments for mobile signatories

- Rationalization of work flows and payment related activities

- Customized printing for cheques

- In short it provides benefit of complete outsourcing of cheque issuance by customers, reducing administrative and operating costs. Cheques are payable at Par on bank's Network with Facsimile signatures of the authorized signatories of the client. Validation is done with the Issuance Data on Date, Amount, Cheque No., and Beneficiary, eliminating any fraudulent encashment.

c. **NEFT/ RTGS/NACH**

The remittance through electronic payment system installed by RBI is through 3 means – NEFT, RTGS and NACH. They are brief described below:

- **National Electronic Funds Transfers (NEFT)**

Individual as well as bulk transfers from one account to many accounts for making payments like distribution of dividend, interest, salary, pension, payment to vendors etc. Customer submits file to the bank containing beneficiary's name, bank name, branch name, account number, IFS Code and amount. Bank uploads the information, debits customer's account and funds are transmitted through RBI to the recipient bank & customer. The turn-around time is less than a day. Branches operating on CBS are able to avail this.

- **Real Time Gross Settlement (RTGS)**

The transaction which happens on NEFT can be done on RTGS if the value of the transaction is not less than Rs. 2 lacs. The turn-around time is much faster as the transfer happens within an hour or so. Banks have to provide funds upfront for settlement as against NEFT where funds are provided on "net" basis.

- **NACH Credit**

NACH Credit is utilized for regular bulk payments like interest, installment, dividend etc., of repetitive nature. The benefit is that information is not required to be given afresh every time. Only changes during the period are required to be incorporated. The remittance is through RBI electronically and the turnaround time is one day. The process involves one time registration of the customer and the recipient. The Company then submits the data in soft form for effecting the transaction. Thus, NACH credit can cater to heavy volume for Payment & Settlement through NPCI in 'error & hassle free' manner.

d. **Payment of Warrants**

This facility renders payments to shareholders/investors for dividend, interest, refund warrants, in physical as well as the electronic modes. The payments are through:

Physical mode comprising of warrants and demand drafts

- Provides on line reconciliation for all the issued interest warrants and list of all unpaid warrants, tallied with outstanding balance can be provided.
- Module inbuilt in CBS
- Scan Image of the paid warrants
- Instrument Level Debits for online Reconciliation
- Paid Unpaid File on Demand/On the internet
- Stop Payment on the warrants issued by the bank
- Bulk processing in short period
- Multiple products processing simultaneously
- Data input through direct uploads
- Payment initiation through web
- Client specific MIS
- MIS download /payment querying through Internet
- Customer can provide the Data centrally in a soft copy. Printing done at payment locations; thus no delivery time
- Bulk Draft issuance in the customized format
- Online access to client for:
  - Payment Initiation & Authorization
  - Stop Payment request

- Beneficiary Upload
- Multi product payment upload through a single file
- Report scheduling
- On Demand Reporting
- Instruction Status Query

- Systems and checks to detect fraudulent encashment and duplicate payments

- Online Validation of Warrants -3 way verification of warrants

  ✓ First, online validation of cheque number, amount and warrant number

  ✓ Second validation of beneficiary name against the master at the time of presenting of warrants.

  ✓ Third, all the above details rechecked against the master on receipt of physical warrants

- Tamper Proof taping of Warrants on amount and beneficiary name on the face of the warrant to obviate risk of fraud due to change in either amount or beneficiary name

- Online access to accounts and transactions

- MIS and Reconciliation Reports –

  - Monthly reconciliation and paid/unpaid reports
  - A final reconciliation report
  - Quarterly reconciliation
  - Balance confirmations

Electronic mode comprising of NEFT, RTGS and NACH

These payments are now increasingly being made through electronic mode. The process is similar for these payments as for other type of payments explained hereinbefore. Banks in addition, arrange to print and send payment advice to the beneficiaries as per customer's requirements.

Key benefits are:

- Payment on due date

- Effortless receipt - No need for visiting Banks for depositing payment cheques

- Avoiding loss of instruments & fraudulent encashment

- Online Validation

- MIS and reconciliation

- Advising the payment advice as per client's business needs and sending the same to the beneficiary through multiple channels like Emails/Courier

e. **Tax payments**

<u>Key Features</u>

- Online Tax – immediate online acknowledgement of the challan

- MIS link showing record of all past payments made, along with the payment status, as well as challan details

- Facility to view, download and print the acknowledged copy of the challan using the MIS option.

- Taxes payable Online:
    - Corporation Tax
    - Service Tax
    - Tax Deducted at Source
    - Income Tax
    - Wealth Tax
    - Central Excise

V. INTERNET BASED CMS SOLUTIONS

- Customers can initiate payment instructions, raise queries on transactions and schedule and view reports through this channel.
- Customers can upload file through their Internet Banking login.
- Bank processes the data and executes instructions.
- Single Sign-on with Internet Banking.

VI. SECURITY

- Banks employ high level of security to ensure security of the data - at three levels – application level, transmission level and server level.
- Application security is through user id and password protection.
- Transmission security is thru 128 bit Secured Socket Layer [SSL] encryption.
- Firewall software and hardware along with password encryption is installed for server security.
- Digital Certificate from VeriSign

VII. BENEFITS OF INTERNET BASED CMS

- 24 X 7 access to banking information

- Payment Initiation from client desk

- Faster Transaction Processing through Single File Upload for all products including RTGS and NEFT

- Comprehensive Data Querying with drill down features

- On Demand Reports / Scheduled Reports,

- Provision to maintain list of designated beneficiaries

- Setting Up of Authorization Verification Matrix of Client Users on the basis of Hierarchy for Transaction Authorization

- Maintenance of Product Wise Accounts

- Maintenance of Users per Client

- Auto derivation of mode of payment from single payment file

- Email Notification to Beneficiaries on transaction cycle completion in case of electronic products

- Anywhere access via the net

- Faster and independent transaction processing through bulk file uploads

- All India single login to bank's Net Banking platform

- A single point of entry for real-time information & transaction

- Solution for online creation or file uploads of payment instructions for execution through varied modes like Cheques, Drafts, RTGS, NEFT & Account Transfers

- Options for instruction level or file level authorization or pre-authorized modes of initiation

- Flexible and scalable authorization matrix permitting multiple authorizing levels

CHAPTER 4

FOREIGN EXCHANGE

I.   PAYMENTS

Banks are required to receive/make payments in foreign currencies on behalf of their customers. These transactions are for various purposes - to meet travel/tour, to meet expenses to stay abroad for study/business or for international trade between two countries.

Every country has laid down laws to regulate these transactions and mostly "authorized dealers" are allowed to deal in foreign currency. This is to ensure that the foreign exchange transactions are kept under control.

In India, a licence from Reserve Bank of India (RBI) is required to be the authorized dealer. There are 4 types of authorized dealers in India – Category I, II, III and Full Fledged Money Changers. Annexure – I contains RBI's notification outlining foreign exchange which can be done by authorized dealers under each category. Further RBI has permitted Authorized Dealers under Category I, Category and FFMCs to appoint Franchisees for carrying on Restricted Money Changing business i.e., conversion of foreign currency notes, coins or traveler's cheques into rupees

The type of transactions largely depends on the purpose and can be categorized primarily in to the following:

- Exchange of foreign currency across the counter
- Foreign Currency Traveler's Cheques
- Credit Cards/Debit Cards (International)

- Prepaid Multi-currency Card
- Remittance through inter-bank channel

i) **Foreign Currency Exchange across Counter**

The travelers across countries carry cash for their petty requirements which they tender for exchange in the country of their visit. Each country has its own rules and regulations, specifying the purpose/maximum amount etc. The currency is required to be tendered to the Authorized Dealer only. Banks form the bulk of such authorized dealers.

For a local bank, foreign currency is like a commodity. It cannot be put in local circulation. Either it can be utilized to issue to another customer who is visiting that country or the currency may have to be shipped to the host country for disposal. Therefore, unless the inflow of a currency matches the outflow, the bank is saddled with idle cash in the form of the said currency. Worse than that, the value of the said amount keeps fluctuating; thus exposing the bank to risk of loss.

As explained above, the balance of foreign currency is independent of the balance in local currency. Accordingly, the bank has to maintain separate accounts for foreign currencies. Given below are examples of accounting entry which a bank would pass for sale and purchase of foreign currency:

EXAMPLE

"A" has to visit Dubai. He wishes to carry USD 500 in cash (permitted as per local regulations). He approaches his bank branch with a request to debit his account and issue the currency to him.

The branch has in its possession 500 USD and accordingly agrees to issue the currency to the customer.

The Process Flow in the bank for the said transaction would be as under:

- The branch will fix the USD/INR (Indian Rupee) exchange rate as per Card Rate notified by banks' Treasury (Mostly, Treasury releases daily card rates for various types of foreign exchange transactions of normal value). Assuming that the Card Rate was INR 47/- per USD, the total amount payable by the Customer would be INR 23,500.

- The balance of foreign currency in the books of the branch (800 USD) is valued at INR 46/- per USD (assumption).

- The branch will pass the following accounting entry:

Customer Account	Debit - 23,500
Foreign Currency Account	Credit- 23,000
Foreign Currency P/L A/c	Credit- 500

The branch would thus make a profit of INR 500.

It would be noticed from the aforementioned that the Foreign Currency Account would be credited at the same rate at which it was debited (without taking into account daily fluctuations – for the sake of simplifying the example). In practice, most of the banks revalue their foreign currency in hand on a daily basis in line with the prevailing market rate for the currency. These rates are advised by the Treasury. In the instant case, the rate at which the Foreign Currency Account entries in the books were made (upon revaluation) immediately prior to the date of aforesaid sale would be the rate applicable at which the account would be credited at the time of sale of the currency. To illustrate, the entries will reflect as under:

a) Accounting entries at the time of purchase of Foreign Currency

Rate: INR 45 per USD

Foreign Currency Account:	Debit - 22,500
Customer Account:	Credit - 21,900
Foreign Exchange P/L A/c:	Credit- 600

(Assuming INR 600 as profit at the time of sale)

b) Rate at the beginning of the day on which sold (for revaluation of the currency based on rate advised by the Treasury) revised to INR 46

Foreign Currency Account	Debit - 500
(46 – 45 i.e., INR 1 per USD)	
Foreign Exchange P/L A/c	Credit - 500

c) At the time of sale @ 47, as shown above, the Foreign Currency Account is credited with 23,000 (thus zeroizing it) and the balance 500 (47-46) is transferred to Foreign Exchange P/L Account.

In case the branch does not have any foreign currency balance, it may purchase the currency from another branch or another authorized dealer. The accounting entries will be accordingly. The fundamental point which will remain applicable to all is that the foreign currency balance is distinct from the local currency balance and its value keeps changing every day based on ruling prices in foreign exchange market.

ii) Foreign Currency Traveler's Cheques

Foreign Currency Traveler's Cheque (FCTC) is a pre-printed, fixed-amount cheque designed to allow the person signing it to make an unconditional payment to someone else as a result of having paid the issuer for that privilege. FCTCs are often used in place of cash by travelers as the name suggests.

London Credit Exchange Company first issued FCTCs in 1772 for use in ninety European cities. In 1874 Thomas Cook had 'circular notes' that operated in the manner of FCTCs. American Express was the first company to develop a large-scale traveler's cheque system in 1891 and is still the largest issuer of traveler's cheques today by volume.

FCTCs are available in several currencies such as USD, Euro, Pound Sterling, Japanese yen, Chinese Yuan, Canadian dollars. They are usually sold in pads of five or ten cheques FCTCs do not expire, so unused cheques can be kept by the purchaser to spend at any time in the future. FCTCs can usually be replaced if lost or stolen (if the owner still has the receipt issued with the purchase of the cheques showing the serial numbers allocated) and they are unpaid till then.

FCTC Companies like American Express, Thomas Cook issue FCTCs while banks (and other Agents) sell them. The buyer of FCTC (Customer) buys it and writes the FCTC in favor of the "Payee" (ME who sold goods/services). FCTC Companies are the issuer and the drawee (obliged to pay) of the FCTCs.

The Customer should immediately append signature on each cheque (usually on the cheque's upper portion) immediately after purchase. In addition, the Customer must safely keep the receipt issued by the Bank for the FCTCs sold by them. The Customer has to countersign (usual on the lower portion) and put the date in the presence of the Payee at the time of delivering FCTC for purchase of goods/services. The Payee is expected to verify identity of the Customer in addition to comparing the existing signatures and those appearing in the identification document.

The FCTC Companies enter into agreement with banks to sell the FCTCs. On the other side, FCTC Companies enter into arrangement with Merchant Establishments (ME) to reimburse to them the value of FCTCs tendered by them to the FCTC Companies for the value of goods sold by them to the FCTC Holder. FCTCs are generally available in most freely exchanged currencies. Banks sell FCTCs to their customers at the prevailing exchange rates plus their commission. The value so received by the banks is credited to the FCTC Companies' accounts at the agreed rates. MEs submit the encashed FCTCs to the FCTC Companies for reimbursement.

FCTC Issuing Process in Banks

- FCTC Company provides FCTC stock to banks for issuing as and when required by the Customer.

- No financial transaction takes place.

- Customer submits request for FCTCs to the Bank.

- Bank debits Customer's Account with the local value of the FCTCs at the rate advised by the Treasury plus commission.

- Bank credits Suspense Account with the amount payable to the FCTC Company and credits Commission to the P/L Account.

- Bank credits FCTC Company's account or issues Pay Order (if no account with the Bank) in favor of the FCTC for the value of FCTCs issued at the rate mutually agreed.

- Bank credits P/L Account with the surplus in Suspense Account (being difference between rate quoted to the Customer and the rate agreed to with the FCTC Company.

EXAMPLE

- Customer buys FCTCs for USD 1000
- Bank quotes INR 47 per USD
- Bank charges INR 500 as Commission
- Bank settles INR 46.50 per USD with the FCTC Company

First set of Entries

Customer Account	Debit	47,500
Suspense FCTC Sale Account	Credit	47,000
P/L Commission	Credit	500

Second set of Entries

Suspense FCTC Sale Account	Debit	47,000
FCTC Company Account OR Pay Order Issue Account	Credit	46,500
P/L FCTC Exchange	Credit	500

FCTC business needs worldwide network of MEs and Banks for facilitating payment and settlement. Therefore, there are only a few international players like American Express and Thomas Cook who offer this service.

FCTC is a safe and easy way to carry money while travelling. Unlike cash, if stolen, the loss can be controlled by immediately reporting the theft over phone, the facility available anywhere around the world. The costs involved in carrying cash as discussed above and the risks of theft associated with the cash are the prime reasons for customers to carry FCTC. In addition, MEs also prefer to avoid cash transactions.

However, with plastic card (Credit and Debit Cards) providing much simpler and on-line facility of payment, FCTC is gradually diminishing in popularity. FCTC is a paper product which requires physical handling. It cannot match speed, accuracy and convenience of electronic medium. Nevertheless, it may still continue to existing for some time to come.

iii) International Credit Cards/Debit Cards

Subject to regulatory guidelines prevailing in different countries, holders of Credit and Debit Cards are now able to conduct international payment transactions. In India these guidelines are now very liberal as they permit use of foreign exchange for various purposes without any approval from any authority. The operations of these Cards are similar to the way it is done for domestic transactions except for the fact that the transaction involves exchange of foreign currency.

The foreign exchange aspect of these cards is explained below:

- The Merchant Establishment is paid by the Acquiring Bank in that country's currency. The Acquiring Bank claims reimbursement in that country's currency from the Credit Card Association (CCA)- RuPay/Visa/ MasterCard/ Amex etc. through which the card has been issued by the bank.

- The conversion of foreign currency transaction in local currency happens at the Card Switch level based at the rate mutually agreed to between the bank and the CCA.

- CCA recovers amount from the card issuing bank in their local currency at the aforesaid mutually agreed rate.

- CCA remits amount to its account in the country where the transaction had taken place and payment was made to the ME (to replenish the balance). The conversion of local currency in to foreign currency thus takes place through the local account of CCA.

- The Credit Card Issuing Company bills the amount to its Cardholder as per billing cycle.

- In case of Debit Cards, the customer account gets debited on-line in local currency.

iv) Prepaid Multi-currency Card

It is named as "World Currency Card", "Global Currency Card", "ForexPlus Card" etc., by different banks in India. It is a prepaid foreign currency card wherein the foreign currency value is loaded into the card. The conversion of local currency into foreign currency happens right at the time of issuance of the card. In other words, it is like foreign currency traveler's cheques; instead of cheques it is a card which offers all the benefits which a card has over paper instrument.

When the card is used, the transaction flows from POS at ME to the bank through Acquiring Bank's switch and CCA's network. The bank debits the balance in the relevant Card Account and sends Authorization back. The ME delivers goods upon receipt of the authorization.

Unlike Credit and Debit Cards (wherein for international transactions, banks reimburse the CCA in local currency), in case of Prepaid Currency Cards, the CCA is reimbursed the amount in the Card Currency. For example, if a bank in India issues a USD Currency Card, the bank provides funds in USD to the CCA for the amount utilized by the customer abroad. In case the utilization is in US, then there is no exchange of currency. CCA gets its US account funded to the amount of USD usage. However, if the usage is in any other currency, the conversion of the currency of that country into USD is taken care of by the CCA and the USD equivalent amount is paid by banks to the CCA.

Key Features

- No loss on account of fluctuations in exchange rate of the currency in which card is taken

- Accepted at all Merchant Establishments worldwide accepting various cards etc.

- Does away with the inconvenience of carrying travelers' cheques

- Safer than carrying foreign currency and travelers' cheques as it is on-line hot listed. Can be replaced with a reloaded card while on travel itself

- More economical than credit cards as the exchange rate is settled upfront

- No need to look for moneychangers – card accepted at thousands of Merchant Establishments

- No transaction fee for shopping abroad

- In India they are available in major currencies - US Dollar, Euro, Sterling Pound, Japanese Yen, Australian Dollar, AED (Dirhams), Canadian Dollar, Singapore Dollar and Swiss Franc

- Banks offer Personal Accident Insurance Covers without additional charges, cover for loss of Checked-in Baggage, Passport Reconstruction Cover etc.

- The primary card can be hot listed in case of loss and balance can be transferred to the issued add on card

- The card can also be used for online purchases / transactions e.g., to pay bills, buy air tickets, do purchases when travelling abroad

- Protection against Foreign Exchange fluctuation – no loss of foreign exchange if used for the same currency in which it has been issued. Transactions however can be done in any currency (exchange rate payable if it is in different currency)

- Card is protected against misuse at ATMs with a PIN. In case the card gets lost or stolen, it has to be reported immediately which can be done through internet

- The card is reloadable even when the cardholder is abroad within the validity period. The reload request can be made by any other person on behalf of the cardholder

- Cardholder can get online access to the card account to track spends, balance and change IPIN

- PIN change can be requested online

- Banks provide monthly statement at mailing address

- Banks are also issuing "chip cards" which has an embedded chip which stores encrypted and confidential information. As compared to magnetic strip cards, this card offers greater security and increased protection against counterfeiting and skimming card frauds

- Instant SMS alerts on all transactions are sent to the customer on his mobile

- On return, the customer can choose to have the balance reimbursed or retain the same for future trips

v)   **Inter-Bank Remittance**

Banks undertake remittance transactions on behalf of its customers - individuals as well as business for their inter-country needs. Like, for individuals it could be (i) for students going abroad for studies (ii) inward remittances from non-resident Indians and (iii) remittance for purchase of goods/ services/assets from abroad etc. Similarly, for importers, manufacturers and exporters, the remittance would be to pay for export and import of goods by them.

Banks create a network of their own branches and correspondent banking relationship with others to facilitate these transactions.

Further the remittance results in currency conversion from remitting country's to recipient country's currency. For example, import from China in to India would mean buying Yuan with Indian Rupees.

Apart from creating payment network, banks have to ensure that these remittances are in compliance of local laws of the land with regard to foreign exchange. For example, in India, the remittances in and out of country are under the control and regulations of Foreign Exchange Management Act (FEMA).

Banks' Payment Network

Banks have options to either open their own branches in various countries or to establishment correspondent business relationship with banks operating in other countries. Once a link is established with a bank in other country, the transactions within that country are possible through that bank who would be a participant in the payment network in that country.

<u>Illustration</u>

To explain that, let us assume that:

- Importer in India imports goods from an Exporter in China and has to make payment to the Exporter.
- Importer has an account with "X" Bank in India.
- Exporter has an account with "Y" Bank in China.
- Importer advises his bank ("X" Bank) to pay to Exporter by crediting his account with "Y" Bank in China.

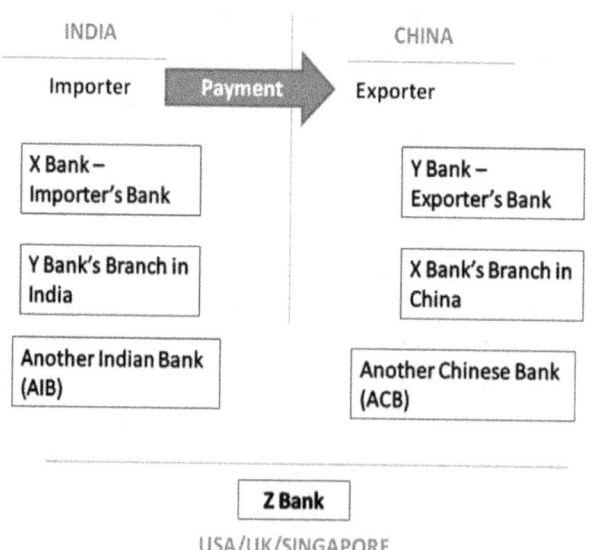

Options for payment by X Bank

i.   "X" Bank may have its own branch in China –

   "X" Bank in India will advise its China branch to pay to "Y" Bank in China. The payment would be in local currency of China i.e., "Yuan" through local clearing/settlement system in China. The settlement between branches of "X" Bank would be as per internal arrangement set up by the Bank.

ii.   "X" Bank may not have its own branch in China but may have its account with "Y" Bank's branch in China#

   "X" Bank will advise "Y" Bank to debit its account for the payment. The transaction will be in Yuan.

   # (In the books of "X" Bank, their account with "Y" Bank would be known as "Nostro" Account. In the books of "Y" Bank, the account of "X" Bank would be known as "Vostro" Account).

iii.   "X" Bank may not have its own branch in China but "Y" Bank may have its account with "X" Bank in India:

   "X" Bank will credit "Y" Bank's account with it for the payment. The transaction will be in local currency of India i.e., Indian Rupees.

iv.   "X" Bank may not have aforesaid (a), (b) and (c) options but may have account with another bank in China ("ACB" Bank) –

   "X" Bank will advise "ACB" Bank to remit money to "Y" Bank for the payment. The transaction will be in local currency of China i.e., Yuan.

v.   "Y" Bank may not have aforementioned arrangements but may have an account with another Bank in India ("AIB" Bank) –

"X" Bank will remit money to "AIB" Bank for crediting "Y" Bank account and will inform "Y" Bank suitably. The transaction will be in local currency of India i.e., Indian Rupees

vi.   "Y" Bank may not have account with "AIB" Bank but "AIB" Bank may have account with "Y" Bank or with any other Bank in China.

"X" Bank will pay to "AIB" Bank who in turn will have the payment made to "Y" Bank either through debit of its Nostro Account or through other bank in China with whom it may have the account

vii.   "X" Bank may route the transaction through its account in a bank in any other financial capital (like US/UK/Singapore) in which city/country, "Y" Bank may also have an account.

"X" Bank will advise its correspondent bank in that city to remit money to "Y" Bank's correspondent bank in that city. The transaction will be in local currency of that country (USD/Euro/Singapore Dollars etc.).

As is evident from the aforesaid, the remitting bank has to look for ways and means to find out a link with the recipient bank so that the required amount is paid on behalf of the importer to the exporter.

Since the remittance involves two countries, it results in conversion of one currency into another irrespective of the currency in which the payment is made. In the aforementioned case of import from China into India, the importer would pay from his rupee account whereas the exporter would receive Yuan. The importer's bank will take rupees from the importer and it or its correspondent bank will buy Yuan from the foreign exchange market to pay to exporter's bank. This buying of Yuan with rupee would be at the rate prevailing in the market at the time of the transaction. And in case, third currency is used to facilitate payment from one country to another (as in last option in the illustration given above); there would be two transactions – one from rupee to USD (if USD is third currency) and second from USD to Yuan.

Like any other market (of goods), the rate depends upon the demand and supply for a particular currency. The demand depends upon international inflows and outflows of the currency. The exchange rate market and mechanism are explained in detail in the following section relating to Trade Finance.

Payment modus operandi

As explained above, under Banks' Payment Network, banks follow different routes to remit funds to other countries depending upon the network created by them. The remittance however involves interaction between remitting branch and the responding branch. This action and response depend upon safe, secured and unambiguous communication. The mode of communication depends upon the type of transaction and the relationship between both entities. It is critical that the message is safe, secured and without any ambiguity. There are several ways in which the remittances are made by the banks:

- Inter-branch Transfer
- Demand Draft
- Electronic (SWIFT)

Inter-branch Transfer

This is where the bank has a branch in both countries. The remitting branch debits customer's account and credits the account of the recipient branch. The Branch may use its in-house messaging system for this inter-branch transfer or may use SWIFT, depending upon internal communication network set up of the bank.

The recipient branch debits the remitting branch and credits the customer (exporter). In case the exporter is having account in some other bank, the transmitting branch sends the remittance through demand draft/electronic mode to that bank.

The amount is arrived at in relation to exchange rate for the currencies of the 2 countries as per internal guidelines of the bank for inter-branch forex transactions, based on inter-bank market rates. In the illustration given earlier, the exchange of currency happens at the branch in China which provides Yuan funds to the exporter.

Demand Draft

If the remittance is by way of a Demand Draft (mostly issued at the request of a customer), the Demand Draft may be issued on bank's own branch abroad. The Demand Draft issuing (remitting) branch debits customer's account and credits Head Office Account of the paying branch (drawee branch). The Demand Draft issuing branch sends intimation to the paying branch through internal messaging system of the bank. Upon receipt of the Demand Draft, paying branch debits Head Office Account of the issuing branch and pays the amount to the payee.

In case the bank does not have its own branch in the other country, the remitting branch draws the Demand Draft on another bank (Correspondent Bank) with whom it has in place the arrangement to draw demand draft. The Correspondent Bank is advised of about the issuance of the Demand Draft.

The customer sends Demand Draft to the payee who deposits the same in his bank in China and gets is paid through clearing settlement system. The draft is paid by the Correspondent Bank when presented for payment by debiting draft issuing bank's account with them.

Electronic

This is the most frequent mode of remittance in banking industry. This requires safe, secure and unambiguous transmission of message. Banks use network of SWIFT (Society for Worldwide Interbank Financial Telecommunication). It is an electronic mode of safe & secured transmission of standardized financial messages. SWIFT is a member-owned cooperative through which the financial world conducts its business operations with speed, certainty and confidence. More than 9,000 banking organizations, securities institutions and corporate customers in 209 countries use it extensively for their financial messages.

SWIFT has devised formats for different types of financial messages. The messages are sent in encrypted codes. Most of the financial messages are formatted and therefore the messages are directly processed with no or very little human intervention. There is a provision for free format message under each of the sub-head (ending with '99') to take care of message not falling within the devised formats.

SWIFT messages consist of five blocks of data including three headers, message content and a trailer. Message types are crucial to identifying content. All SWIFT messages include the prefix "MT" (Message Type). This is followed by a 3-digit number that denotes the message type, category, and group. Given below is the overview of the SWIFT MT categories:

Message Type	Description
MT0xx	System Messages
MT1xx	Customer Payments and Cheques
MT2xx	Financial Institution Transfers
MT3xx	Treasury Markets
MT4xx	Collection and Cash Letters
MT5xx	Securities Markets
MT6xx	Treasury Markets - Metals and Syndications
MT7xx	Documentary Credits and Guarantees
MT8xx	Travelers Cheques
MT9xx	Cash Management and Customer Status

Format MT 202 - for Financial Institution Transfers – Key Points

- MT 202 is primarily used for Financial Institution transfers and referred to as the traditional Swift MT202

- MT 202 is also used as a Cover message for transfers to beneficiary banks for ultimate credit to beneficiary banks already in receipt of MT103 client credit information. The MT103 is sent directly to the beneficiary bank whilst the funds transfer flows through Bank to Bank transfers (MT 202)

- The current cover message MT 202 provides no underlying beneficiary nor ordering customer information

- MT 202 COV, the new message format, incorporates ordering party information and beneficiary details to prevent money laundering and terrorist access to wire transfers in compliance of FATF guidelines.

- Originating Institutions must ensure that qualifying wire transfers contain complete originator and beneficiary information and also verify information for accuracy and maintain info according to FATF standards

- Originating Institutions must use appropriate SWIFT message for all cover messages per SWIFT User Handbook

- Intermediary Financial Institution for both domestic and cross border wire transfers must ensure that complete originator information accompanies each wire transfer and that wire transfers retain all original information

MT 202 General Financial Institution Transfer Format

SWIFT: MT 202		
Field	**M/O**	**Tag**
Transaction Reference Number	M	20
Related Reference	M	21
Time Indication	OR	13C
Value Date / Currency Code / Amount	M	32A
Ordering Institution	O	52A
Sender's Correspondent	O	53A
Receiver's Correspondent	O	54A
Intermediary	O	56A
Account with Institution	O	57A
Beneficiary Institution	M	58A
Sender to Receiver Information	O	72

vi) **Regulatory compliance**

The payments/receipts from one country to another are subject to regulatory provisions prevailing in both the countries. Unlike domestic remittances, it is therefore important that due checks and balances are in place for controlling/regulating such payments/receipts. In India, all foreign exchange inflows and outflows are controlled and regulated under Foreign Exchange Management Act (FEMA). Banks are required to follow provisions of the Act and the guidelines issued by Reserve Bank of India (RBI) from time to time.

Banks have to report all transactions to RBI periodically.

Financial Action Task Force (FATF)

FATF is an inter-governmental body whose purpose is the development and promotion of national and international policies to combat money laundering and terrorist financing. The FATF is therefore a "policy-making body" created in 1989 that works to generate the necessary political will to bring about legislative and regulatory reforms in these areas.

Guidelines have been issued with the objective of preventing terrorists and other criminals from having unfettered access to wire transfers for moving their funds and for detecting such misuse when it occurs. The core requirement of this regulation is that the Payments Service Provider (A natural or legal person whose business includes the provision of transfer of funds services) is to ensure that all electronic payments, both incoming and outgoing, carry specified information about the originator (the Payer) of the instruction. Complete payer information needs to accompany transfer of funds which consists of –

- Account number (or unique identifier if an account number does not exist)

- Name

- Address

vii) Other Forex Transactions

a. Foreign Inward Remittances

When an individual, a firm, a company, a trust or any other organization receives funds from any foreign country through banking channels, it is termed as Foreign Inward Remittance. Foreign inward remittances can be in the form of demand drafts, electronic funds transfers, cheques, travelers' cheques, foreign currency notes, foreign postal orders, international money orders etc.

As per the Foreign Exchange Management Act (FEMA), 1999, before undertaking any transaction in foreign exchange on behalf of any person, the Bank can ask that person to give suitable declarations / such information required to reasonably satisfy the Bank that the transaction is not or will not involve any contravention or evasion of the provisions of the FEMA 1999, or any rules, regulations etc. issued thereunder.

Issue of Bank Certificate (FIRC)

Forward Inward Remittance Certificates (FIRC) in form BCI should be issued against receipt of inward remittances or realization of foreign exchange. Such certificates should not be issued for inward remittances received for credit to NRE or FCNR accounts as the funds in these accounts are repatriable.

Authorized / Designated Branches

As per the guidelines of the Reserve Bank of India, the branches / offices of banks are classified into the following three categories for the purpose of transacting foreign exchange business.

Category 'A': Offices and branches maintaining independent foreign currency accounts in their names.

Category 'B': Offices and branches not maintaining independent foreign currency accounts but having powers of operating on the accounts maintained abroad by Corporate Office.

Category 'C': All other offices and branches handling foreign exchange business through category A or category B offices or branches.

b. Foreign Inward DDs and Electronic Transfers

Demand Drafts (DDs) and Electronic / Telegraphic Transfers (EFTs/TTs) are drawn on banks in India sent by foreign correspondents. The services for inward remittances (DDs and EFTs/TTs) drawn by correspondents abroad are provided through Category 'A' & 'B' branches.

Rates of exchange for purchase of currency depends upon prevailing market rates notified by the Treasury. When there is a forward exchange contract, the contracted rate should be applied after ensuring that the transaction is within the validity period of the contract.

Commission and other charges for inward remittances are recovered as per bank's internal guidelines of the Bank.

Bank credits account of the customers after verifying that the relative amount / funds (cover) has been received in the Nostro account.

Unless indicated to the contrary on the face of the drafts or in the relative schedule of arrangements, drafts issued by foreign banks should be considered as stale after six months from the date of issue and a reference should be made to the issuing bank before paying such a draft.

Bank has to ensure that the purpose of the remittance is in consonance with the purposes authorized under FEMA i.e., whether it represents transfer of capital, savings, gift, profits dividend etc. should be indicated and reported in the supplementary statement

c.   Collection of foreign clean bills, cheques etc.

Banks send foreign instruments - cheques, dividend warrants, demand drafts, travelers' cheques and other clean instruments expressed in foreign currency and payable outside India for collection to correspondent banks in those countries as per arrangement with them. For example, a US Dollar draft drawn on London (UK) should be sent for collection directly to London. The correspondent bank is instructed to remit /credit the proceeds in the Nostro account of the collecting Bank maintained in the currency of the instrument to avoid loss of exchange unless of course where the bank does not have a nostro account in that country.

Credit to the customer is given upon receipt of credit of the instruments in the Nostro account after deducting commission and charges. Where as per the arrangement with local representative of foreign correspondent, credit to our Nostro account is given subject to final payment, the credit is given to the customer only when the reserve period   for return of instruments is over and the credit becomes irrevocable.

In case of forged / fraudulent instruments, the reserve period is unlimited, i.e., the foreign correspondent can reverse the credit at any time after the forgery/fraud is detected. The Bank's right to debit the customer's account any time in such cases should be brought to the notice of the customer.

On receipt of information of return of cheque, appropriate returning fee is recovered from the customer. Foreign correspondent's charges, if any are also recovered.

Purchase of Instruments

Purchasing a foreign currency instrument exposes the Bank to credit risk as the instruments sent for collection may be returned unpaid. Purchase of instruments is, therefore, undertaken only for the customers having such credit limits.

Purchasing of foreign currency cheques, dividend warrants, demand drafts etc., is to be done at Bill Buying Rate and travelers' cheques at TC Buying Rate. The instruments are sent for collection to foreign correspondents as per the usual procedure.

In case the purchased instrument is subsequently returned unpaid, recovery of amount is effected at TT selling rate ruling on the date of recovery together with interest/overdue interest. The charges levied by the foreign correspondent are also recovered.

Collection of Instruments Drawn in Foreign Currency Payable at Other Banks in India

Instruments drawn in foreign currency payable at other banks in India are sent direct to the drawee bank's branch for collection. The drawee branch is advised to remit the proceeds by banker's cheque / draft.

In cases where:

- The remittance or part of remittance is meant for credit to FCNR, EEFC or other foreign currency accounts, or

- The amount of the instrument is large (say over US $ 25,000) and the Bank apprehensive about not getting a competitive exchange rate by the drawee bank,

The drawee is advised to remit the proceeds by credit to Nostro account of the bank abroad in the currency of the instrument. On receipt of advice of credit, the procedure as in case of collection of foreign instruments is followed to credit amount to the customer's account.

Alternatively, the drawee bank is advised to send a counter draft for the proceeds of the instruments, drawn in the currency of the instrument and payable in the country of the currency of the instrument. Such counter draft, on receipt, it is sent for collection to bank's correspondent abroad.

Collection of Instruments Drawn in Rupees Payable at Other Banks in India

Instruments drawn in rupees payable at other banks in India are sent for collection by following the procedure as in case of inland cheques, bills etc. for collection. The drawee bank issues Foreign Inward Bank Certificate (FIRC) and sends it to the bank for passing on to the customer. On realization of proceeds, the customer's account can be credited after deducting our usual charges.

d. Encashment of Foreign Currency TCs

Encashment of foreign currency travelers' cheques from public and accountholders can be carried out by all Authorized branches may encash travelers' cheques of foreign correspondents

The following categories of persons generally approach the Bank for encashment of travelers' cheques:

- Foreign Travelers and Non-Resident Indians visiting India.

- Indian residents to whom foreign exchange had been released in the form of travelers' cheques surrendering the balance left with them.

- Authorized money changers like Hotels, Shops etc. who had received these in payment of their sales / services.

- Full-fledged authorized money changers.

Encashment of foreign currency travelers' cheques is fraught with certain risks. Fraudulent encashment of travelers' cheques from the 'Lost/ stolen' is one such major risk.

Salient features (illustrative) of guidelines for scrutiny and payment of travelers' cheques given below:

- The encashing official should take maximum care to see that the travelers' cheques presented are genuine (bonafide), by referring to the security features as per details supplied, including comparing the specimen provided by the respective travelers' cheques issuing institutions.

- Blank travelers' cheques, i.e., cheques which were not signed by the purchaser at the space for original (holder's) signature ('When countersigned below with this signature') at the time of purchasing them, should not be accepted for encashment. The fact that the cheques are blank and the procedure for their issuance to the purchaser has not been properly followed is an indication that the person presenting them for encashment may not be the person who purchased the cheques.

- It should be ensured that the cheques presented are not already countersigned at the place where it is specified on the cheque 'Countersign here in the presence of person cashing', except where presented by a third party like Hotels, Shop etc., with whom a formal arrangement is entered into by the Bank. In rare cases where the cheques already countersigned, are required to be paid, the customer should be requested to sign on the back of the cheque.

- Also proof of identification such as passport / driving licence etc. should be verified and recorded.

- The travelers' cheques should be verified by placing under an ultra-violet ray machine. It should be made sure that original signature made at 'When countersigned below with this Signature', does not appear to have been erased, or does not appear to have been written over with felt tip pen (i.e., signatures with broad strikes).

- The holder should sign in the presence of the paying official who must carefully compare the second signature / counter signature with the original signature on the travelers' cheques to ensure that both the signatures are exactly the same and there is no variation in the signatures.

- The passport of the presenter of the travelers' cheques should be scrutinized to establish her/his identity. It must be ensured that the photograph in the passport is of the person encashing the travelers' cheques. Photo copies of the relevant pages of the passport indicating passport number, place of issue, date of issue, expiry date of the passport, entry visa particulars etc. of the encasher should be held on.

- In case of doubt, reference should be made on phone to the issuing institution's international 24 hours help line (a Collect Call)

Travelers' cheques are purchased by applying TC Buying Rate given in daily rate schedule by the Treasury.

Unlike other commercial transactions, which are not conducted on Saturdays owing to non-availability of exchange rates, travelers' cheques are encashed on Saturdays from foreign tourists by applying the exchange rate advised by the Treasury.

Process for Collection / Claiming Reimbursement

The travelers' cheques are sent to the correspondent bank (or their representative office in India, as per arrangement) with whom the bank maintains Nostro account in the concerned currency, as is done in case of collection of other foreign currency instruments. The travelers' cheques may also be instead sent to Local Office of travelers' cheques issuing company as per the arrangement in this regard.

The other related formalities / guidelines given in Part - 'C', 'Collection of Foreign Clean Bills, Cheques etc.' are followed.

Encashment Certificates

Tourists encashing travelers' cheques, may request for issuance of encashment certificate. Encashment certificates may be issued by the bank incorporating details of the cheques encashed and the holder's name, passport number etc.

Travelers' cheques can be purchased from customers as well as good merchant establishments and hotels etc. who come into possession of such travelers' cheques in the normal course of business, provided they are duly countersigned and signatures appear in order. A letter of indemnity is obtained from them undertaking, inter alia, to reimburse the bank with the amount of any travelers' cheques purchased from them and returned subsequently by the issuers for any reasons whatsoever.

e. Purchase of Foreign Currency Notes

Purchase of foreign currency notes can be undertaken by all Category 'B' branches for non-customers (walk-in business) as well as regular customers of the Bank. The identity of the person encashing the currency should be properly established by verification of passport and noting full address (local and permanent) etc. on record and observing other normal precautions as in case of encashment of travelers' cheques.

Currency Declaration Form

Person tendering currency is required to declare in Currency Deposit Form (CDF) in respect of foreign currency brought in by them where the aggregate value of bank notes, foreign currency notes and travelers' cheques exceeds as stipulated under FEMA.

Currencies for Purchase

Foreign currency notes expressed in currencies advised by the Treasury on the rates given in the daily rate card is applied for the purchase.

Encashment Certificates

Encashment Certificate is issued in all cases of purchase of foreign currency from the public, irrespective of whether CDF has been submitted or not by the tenderer of foreign exchange and whether the tenderer asks for the certificate or not.

Shipping crew members encashing foreign currency (and travelers' cheques) representing their salaries, should be issued a certificate in form 10 H to enable them to submit it to the Income Tax authorities along with Return of

Income. No separate ECF form should be submitted in such cases.

The certificates should not be issued for inward remittance received for credit to NRE or FCNR accounts as the funds in these accounts are repatriable.

Only one certificate should be issued for each remittance received.

If the inward remittance is received through another bank in India, the certificate must be obtained from that bank (in India) on which the instrument is drawn.

Disposal of (Excess) Currency Notes

Foreign currency notes encashed or received for collection is disposed of two authorized money changers at mutually agreed rates. The exchange difference (between paid to the customer and received from the money changer) is credited to Profit & Loss Account.

The transaction is reported as purchase of foreign currency.

Holding Stock of Foreign Currency Notes

Bank may hold stock of foreign currency notes to meet sale requirements for its customers.

A currency-wise 'Foreign Cash Accounts (US Dollars/ GBP etc.)' is maintained.

Every Purchase or sale transaction of foreign currency notes handled during the day is reported separately to Treasury Department.

The balances held in foreign currency notes is shown as foreign currency cash balance in the books.

Evaluation / Revaluation of Stock of Foreign Currency Notes on Hand

The stock of foreign currency notes is required to be evaluated at the market rate. Necessary entries are be passed by debiting/crediting P & L Account Exchange (Foreign) and 'G/L Account Foreign Cash on Hand' is adjusted accordingly.

f.   Foreign Outward Remittances

Foreign outward remittances involve sale of foreign exchange. Banks (ADs) can sell foreign exchange in accordance with the relative provisions of Foreign Exchange Management Act (FEMA), 1999, the rules, regulations etc. framed thereunder and RBI guidelines.

Foreign outward remittance can be classified into two basic categories:

a.   Remittances for import of goods into country (The relevant guidelines of Trade Finance should be followed in case of outward remittances pertaining to imports), and

b.   those for purposes other than import of goods.

Types of Remittances

Foreign outward remittance can be effected in any of the following modes:

a)   Demand Drafts
b)   Electronic/ Telegraphic Transfers (SWIFT/ Telex)
c)   Travelers' Cheques
d)   Currency Notes

Application for Remittance

Persons, firms and banks (other than Authorized Dealers) making remittances in any foreign currency to a beneficiary abroad are required to apply to the Bank (Authorized Dealer) on forms separately prescribed for import and for other cases.

As per the FEMA 1999, before undertaking any transaction in foreign exchange on behalf of any person, the Bank can ask that person to give suitable declarations / such information required to reasonably satisfy the Bank that the transaction is not or will not involve any contravention or evasion of the provisions of the FEMA 1999, or any rules, regulations etc. issued thereunder. Banks are required to follow guidelines issued by RBI which, inter-alia, require banks to keep on record any information / documentation on the basis of which the transaction was undertaken for verification by the RBI. If a person (applicant) refuses to comply with any such requirement, the branches can refuse to undertake the transaction. If the branch has reason to believe that any contravention / evasion is contemplated by the person, it is required to report the matter to RBI.

Banks are required to verify and certify the correctness of the statements made in the application and its enclosures and to ensure that they are complete in all respects and are signed by the applicant.

Remittances for current transactions which, under the FEMA 1999, Rules, are not specifically prohibited or which do not require prior approval of Government of India or Reserve Bank of India may be permitted by the Bank without any monetary / percentage ceilings subject to compliance with other related provisions.

Rates of exchange for outward remittance by way of demand drafts, electronic/ telegraphic transfers, sale of travelers' cheques or foreign currency notes as given by Treasury are applied. Commission and other charges for outward remittances are recovered as per internal guidelines of the Bank.

Manner of Payment of Rupees Against Sale of Foreign Exchange

The payment must be received through bank account. No remittances should be effected unless the Bank has received equivalent Indian rupees.

g. Sale of Foreign Exchange for Travel

The traveler should be in possession of a valid passport authorizing travel to the countries proposed to be visited as well as ticket for travel to the country /countries for which exchange has been applied for. The ticket held by the traveler should have been issued for a journey commencing within a reasonable period (say sixty days) from the date of sale of foreign exchange.

Foreign exchange can be released for visits for various purposes to Bangladesh/ Myanmar / Pakistan by land route without production of journey tickets.

Exchange may be sold as per the permissible limit on the basis of a declaration given by the traveler regarding the amount of foreign exchange availed of during a calendar year.

Out of the overall foreign exchange being sold to a traveler, exchange in the form of foreign currency notes and coins may be sold up to amount as specified by RBI from time to time.

In case the foreign exchange purchased for any purposes is not used for the purposes or for any other purpose for which purchase or acquisition of foreign exchange is permitted under the provision of FEMA 1999 or Rules or Regulations made thereunder, the unused portion is required to be surrendered to an authorized person within the specified period.

Unspent foreign exchange brought back to India by a traveler is required to be surrendered to an authorized person against payment in rupees.

Remittances for Tour Arrangements etc.

Banks may remit foreign exchange to travelers towards their hotel accommodation, tour arrangement etc. (including exchange drawn for private travel abroad) in the countries proposed to be visited by them provided it is out of the foreign exchange purchased by the traveler from the authorized dealer in accordance with the Rules, Regulations and Directions in force.

Banks may effect remittances at the request of agents in India who have tie-up arrangements with hotels / agents, etc., abroad for providing hotel accommodations or making other tour arrangements for travelers from India, provided they are satisfied that the remittance is being made out of the foreign exchange purchased by the concerned traveler from an authorized person (including exchange drawn for private travel abroad) in accordance with the Exchange Control Rules, Regulations and Directions in force.

h. International Credit Cards

Banks or their subsidiaries in India do not require permission from RBI from exchange control angle for issue of ICCs to residents

Returning Indians maintaining Resident Foreign Currency (RFC) Accounts in India or Foreign Currency Accounts abroad can also use ICCs freely without any end-use restrictions provided the reimbursements are made by debit to their RFC accounts in India or foreign currency accounts held abroad.

Non-residents are free to nominate any resident as additional / add-on card holder. The claims arising out of such cards should be met by the non-residents from their foreign currency accounts maintained in India or abroad.

If the additional / add-on card has been arranged by a NRI, the claims against the card may be met from the NRIs' NRE / FCNR account held in India also.

However, no remittance from India by the resident add-on cardholder is permitted for settlement of claims against such additional / add-on credit cards.

EEFC facility is not available to the recipients in respect of payments received from residents against ICCs.

RBI issues guidelines in respect of the aforesaid which banks have to refer to from time to time and ensure strict compliance.

i. DDs and Electronic Funds Transfers

Demand drafts (DDs) are issued only on foreign correspondent bank with which bank has agency arrangement. DDs are issued in accordance with the terms of the respective agency agreements. Normally the drafts are to be drawn only on the branch of the correspondent bank where Nostro account is maintained and in the currency of the Nostro account.

The purpose of the remittance is to be eligible for remittance as per extant exchange regulations.

An advice of drawing is sent by SWIFT to the correspondent bank.

Charges of correspondent bank are recovered from the customer along with banks DD issue charges.

Cancellation of Demand Draft Issued

At the request of a customer, a foreign currency draft may be cancelled after being satisfied about the reasons for cancellation. The correspondent bank on whom the draft was drawn is advised of the cancellation. Such a transaction represents a purchase of foreign currency and the rupee amount is refunded to the applicant by converting the foreign currency at the TT buying rate.

Demand draft forms and travelers' cheques are to be treated like cash and are should be stored in a fireproof safe under dual control. As soon as the stocks are received, they should be entered in Foreign Draft / Travelers' Cheques stock record.

Electronic/ Telegraphic Transfers (Swift)

Electronic/ Telegraphic Transfers (EFT/ TT) are normally issued through correspondent bank with which banks have SWIFT authentication facility.

Where the EFT/ TT is sent through a correspondent bank with whom bank does not maintain Nostro account in the currency of EFT, the correspondent bank with whom the bank is maintaining the Nostro account in the currency of remittance is advised to fund the paying bank.

j.   Sale of Travelers' Cheques

The guidelines for 'Sale of Foreign Exchange for Travel' apply to sale TCs as well. The safekeeping guidelines for TCs are similar to those for DDs

Travelers' cheques of the banks / institutions with which bank has entered into arrangements are issued as per the terms and conditions of the respective arrangements.

Issuance of foreign currency travelers' cheques to the public and account holders can be carried out by all Category 'B' branches and other branches specifically authorized for the purpose.

Issuance of Travelers' Cheques (TC)

Following forms, duly filled in and signed, should be obtained from a purchaser of TCs:

- A request for issue of TC
- Purchaser's Application Form, supplied by the bank / institution whose TCs are being issued
- Exchange Control declaration

The Bank's rubber stamp with the official's initials should be put on the reverse of the TCs. The purchaser's signature must be obtained on the face of the TCs in the space provided in presence of the bank official. The official should initial the TC Issued Register in token of having verified the signature and endorsed the passport, permit (where applicable).

An acknowledgement for receipt of the travelers' cheques is obtained from the applicant in the Register and on the Purchase Slip.

Rate of Exchange and Commission

TCs are sold at the TC Selling Rate for the respective foreign currency ruling on the date of sales, plus commission (as advised by the bank from time to time).

Cover for Sales

Cover for sales of travelers' cheques is effected by remitting foreign currency concerned in favor of the bank / institution whose travelers' cheques have been issued or as per the agreed arrangement in this regard. The sale is reported to Treasury.

k.   Sale of Foreign Currency Notes

Sale of foreign currency notes can be undertaken by banks for customers as well as non-customers

The guidelines for 'Sale of Foreign Exchange for Travel' apply for sale of foreign currency as well. For providing foreign currency travelers' cheques and notes to the Master /Captain of foreign vessels against inward remittance, the related FEMA provisions/RBI guidelines are to be referred to.

Re-conversion of Indian Currency

The Bank may sell foreign currency against Indian rupees held by persons who are not residents of India but are passing through or leaving India after a visit, at the time of their departure from India, provided a bank / encashment certificate issued on the prescribed form by an authorized dealer, exchange bureau or authorized money changer is produced to show that the rupee had been acquired by sale of foreign exchange to an authorized dealer or money changer in India and the certificate is valid for such re-conversion.

The sale of currency is reported to Treasury as in case of reporting merchant transactions.

I. World Currency Card/Global Card

Persons travelling abroad need foreign currency to meet expenses in the foreign country. Under FEMA they are allowed to carry an equivalent of USD 10000 per annum and USD 25000 per trip for personal and business trips respectively. They carry this in the form of currency notes or Traveler's cheques. Alternatively, they can use their Debit/ credit cards.

In addition, banks now offer prepaid debit card in foreign currency. The customer has to load this card with the required foreign currency amount which can be drawn through ATMs and POS terminals in countries other than India, Nepal and Bhutan. The product is called World Currency Card/Global Currency Card etc.

The cards are available in different currencies – US Dollars (USD), Pound Sterling (GBP), Euro (EUR), Australian Dollar

(AUD), Canadian Dollar (CAD), Singapore Dollar (SGD) etc. Each bank has its own range.

The applicant has to submit details like Name, DOB, address, telephone number, email id, mobile number, passport details, ticket number etc.) and submit documents like copy of the Passport, copy of the air ticket, PAN Number and other supporting documents for travel.

Reload of World Currency Cards

- Reloads can be done only during the validity of the card.

- It can be reloaded only to the extent permitted by FEMA from time to time.

- Only the original applicant or in case of Corporate Card the duly authorized person can request for a reload.

Refund of World Currency Cards amount

- The original purchaser of World currency card only can apply for the refund.

- Refund is to be made by way of A/c payee pay-order, credit to the customer's account or purchase of new world currency card.

- The card has to be hot-listed immediately

- The cancellation of WCC is a purchase of foreign exchange by the bank Replacements of WCC

Replacement is done in case of loss of card on the request of the customer. The Card is immediately hot-listed. The new card is handed over or sent to the customer through courier. The charges (replacement card fee and courier) are recovered by debit to the card account.

II. EXCHANGE RATE MECHANISM

i) Rates of Exchange

The rate at which one currency is converted into another currency is called exchange rate. The exchange rate can be quoted in following two ways.

- Direct Quotations - In direct quotations, the price of counter currency is expressed as a certain number of units of that local currency per unit of US $ (or the base currency).

  E.g., US $ 1 = Rs 46.4825

- Indirect Quotations - In indirect quotations, the rates are quoted as a certain number of units of US $ (or the base currency) per unit of local currency.

  E.g., Rs 100 = US $ 2.1525

In India, direct quotations are used. The exchange rate for Indian Rupee is quoted against one unit of foreign currency, except the following currencies for which exchange rates are quoted against 100 units of foreign currencies:

- Belgian Franc
- Japanese Yen
- Indonesian Rupiah
- Kenyan Shillings
- Spanish Peseta

Base Currency

In foreign exchange transactions, it is necessary to know which currency is being bought or sold. The currency which is being bought or sold is known as 'Base Currency'. In a quote, the first currency (currency at the left) is the base currency.

Basis Point / Pip

One basis point is the last decimal in the quotation of an exchange rate.

For example, in US $ 1 = CHF 1.7135, 5 is known as a point or a Pip.

One basis point is 0.01 percent when referring to interest rates or yield.

ii)   Two Way Quotations - Bid and Offer

In foreign exchange market, it is a practice to always quote two way rates i.e., the rate for buying (bid) as well as for selling (offer). The quotations are given in the ascending order. The first rate / lower rate is the bid rate. The second / higher rate is the offer rate. For example, when a bank quotes US $ 1 = (INR) 46.4825 - 46.4875, it means that the bank is ready to deal in USD and would buy USD at Rs 46.4825 and sell USD at Rs 46.4875.

The difference between bid (buying) and offer (selling) rates is known as spread.

It is a convention that the rates are quoted by giving the first rate in full and only last two digits of the other. For example, the rates mentioned earlier are quoted as:

1 US $ = (INR) 46.4825 /75

To save time, participants in foreign exchange market, often quote the rates by giving only last two digits, as it is presumed that the other figures are known. The above mentioned rates may thus be quoted as 25/75. Incidentally, the figure 48 (in US $ = 1 NR 46.4825/75) is known as "Big figure".

iii)   Cross Rates

In case, the price of one currency is not quoted against the other currency, the parity between them is decided by using an intermediary currency. The rate thus obtained is called a Cross Rate and the principle applied to obtain the cross rate is called the Chain Rule.

- If US Dollar is quoted in India at US $ 1 = Rs 46.6675 / 6725 and SGD is quoted as US $ 1 = SGD 1.7925/75, then the rate at which the Bank can buy SGD against Rupee can be calculated as follows:

  Buy US $ at their offer rate US $ 1 = Rs 46.6725

  Buy SGD against US $ i.e., Sell US $ at their bid rate US $ 1 = SGD 1.7925

  US $ 1 = SGD 1.7925

  SGD 1 = US $ 1/1.7925

  US $ 1 = Rs 46.6725

  Therefore, SGD 1 = 46.6725/1.7925

  SGD 1 = Rs 26.0375

- Similarly, the rate at which the Bank can sell SGD and receive Rupee can be calculated as follows:

  Buy US $ at their offer rate US $ 1 = SGD 1.7975

  Sell US $ at their bid rate US $ 1 = Rs 46.6675

US $ 1 = SGD 1.7975

SGD 1 = US $ 1/1.7975

US $ 1 = Rs 46.6675

Therefore, SGD 1 = 46.6675/1.7975

SGD 1 = 25.9625

iv) Buying Selling Rate

As all purchase / sale transactions are not alike, there are different buying and selling rates. The principle involved is that an instrument / transaction involving little expense (work / effort) and risk will be more valuable i.e., it will command a better price for the seller than an instrument costing more to collect and involving greater risk.

Various types of rates for different (merchant) transactions are:

- TT Selling Rate
- Bill Selling Rate
- TT Buying Rate
- Bill Buying Rate

The rates as given in the table below are quoted / applied depending on the nature of the transactions unless a forward contract is booked by the customer which he desires to use. In that case, forward contract rate will be applicable within the validity period and for the specific transaction in the contract.

Selling Rates	Buying Rates
T.T. Selling Rate i) Clean outward remittance (TT, MT, DD) in foreign currency ii) Cancellation of purchase made in foreign currency: a) Bill purchased earlier is returned unpaid b) Bill purchased earlier transferred to collection account / crystallized bills. c) Earlier inward remittance (converted into rupees) is refunded to the remitting bank. iii) Crystallization of bills.	T.T. Buying Rate i) Clean inward remittances (TT, MT, DD) for which cover has already been provided by credit to the Nostro account of the Bank. ii) Realization of proceeds instruments sent for collection. iii) Cancellation of outward TT, MT, DD, etc.
iv) Cancellation of forward purchase contracts.	iv) Cancellation of forward sales contracts.
Bill Selling Rate Retirement of import bills received under letters of credit or for collection.	Bill Buying Rate Purchase/ negotiation (under letter of credit) of export bills in foreign currency.

Apart from the above rates, banks usually quote the following rates:

- Travelers' Cheques Selling Rate

- Foreign Currency Notes Selling Rate
- Clean Cheques Buying Rate
- Travelers' Cheques Buying Rate
- Foreign Currency Notes Buying Rate

v)   Value Date

As it takes some time to process transactions and send instructions, in foreign exchange market it is a practice to quote a rate for a deal, but exchange the currencies at a later date. The date on which such actual cash flows take place/currencies are exchanged is called Value Date. Based on this concept of value date, following types of exchange rates are quoted in the Market:

Type of Deal	Term for Exchange of Currency / Cash Flow	Example	
		Date of the Deal	Value Date
i) Value Today / Cash /Ready	Same Day	14/1/2011 (Friday)	14/1/2011 (Friday)
ii) Value Tomorrow/ Tom	Next Working Day	14/1/2011 (Friday)	17/1/2011 (Monday)
iii) Spot	2nd Working Day	14/1/2011 (Friday)	18/1/2011 (Tuesday)
iv) Forward	At an agreed date beyond spot	14/1/2011 (Friday)	Beyond 18/1/2011

vi)   Forward Exchange Rate

The exchange rate for settlement beyond spot date is called forward rate. Forward rate has two components:

a.   Spot Rate

b.   Forward Point or Forward Differential (Premium or Discount)

Forward differential represents the interest differential between the pair of currencies provided capital flows are freely allowed. As rupee convertibility is subject to exchange control regulations for free movement of capital to and from India, in case of US $ / Rupee the demand and supply determines the forward differentials (points).

Forward rates are quoted by indicating spot rate and premium or discount. In direct quotations:

Forward Rate = Spot Rate + Premium or - Discount.

If the currency is costlier (ascending) in future (forward) as compared to spot, it is said to be at a premium in relation to another currency. The premium is added to both buying and selling rate.

If the currency is cheaper (descending) in future (forward) as compared to spot, it is said to be at discount in relation to another currency. The discount is always deducted from both buying and selling rate.

It may be clarified that it is the base currency for which the premium or discount is always mentioned.

vii)   Rate for Option Forward Contracts

Option forward contract provides for a delivery of the contract during a specified period in future. The rates charged to the customers for option forward contracts are calculated on the assumption that the customer delivers the exchanges, or asks for its delivery, on the day which is the least favorable from the Bank's point of view.

Thus, if forward rates are quoted at a discount, the Bank takes the view that sale transaction would be put through by the customer at the earliest and therefore, quote the least discount. In a purchase transaction, the Bank takes into account the latest date of delivery by the customer, to take maximum discount.

If the forward rates are quoted at premium, the Bank takes the view that the sale transaction would be put through by the customer at the latest date and accordingly charge the maximum premium. In a purchase transaction, the customer may effect delivery at his earliest and the Bank therefore, gives least premium.

viii)   Swap

Buying and selling or selling and buying simultaneously for the same amount and same currency for different value dates is called 'Swap'. A swap could be spot /forward, forward / forward, cash/spot, tom/spot, cash/tom, cash/ forward, or tom/ forward.

For example:

> Buy spot / sell forward, or
> Buy forward / sell forward
> > Or

Sell spot / buy forward, or
Sell forward / buy forward.
Or
Buy cash / sell spot, or
Buy tom / sell spot.

Annexure I

Categories of Authorized Dealers

Category	Entities	Major Activities
Category - I	• Commercial Banks • State Co-op Banks • Urban Co-op Banks	All current and capital account transactions according to RBI directions issued from time-to-time.
Category - II	• Upgraded FFMCs • Co-op. Banks • Regional Rural Banks (RRBs) • Others	Specified non-trade related current account transactions mentioned below as also all the activities permitted to Full Fledged Money Changers and any other activity as decided by the Reserve Bank: a) Private Visits, b) Remittance by tour operators / travel agents to overseas agents / principals / hotels, c) Business Travel, d) Fee for participation in global conferences and specialized training,

		e) Remittance for participation in international events / competitions (towards training, sponsorship and prize money).
		f) Film shooting
		g) Medical Treatment abroad
		h) Disbursement of crew wages
		i) Overseas Education
		j) Remittance under educational tie up arrangements with universities abroad
		k) Remittance towards fees for examinations held in India and abroad and additional score sheets for GRE, TOEFL etc.
		l) Employment and processing, assessment fees for overseas job applications
		m) Emigration and Emigration Consultancy Fees

		n) Skills / credential assessment fees for intending migrants o) Visa fees, p) Processing fees for registration of documents as required by the Portuguese / other Governments q) Registration / Subscription / Membership fees to International Organizations
Category - III	Select Financial and other Institutions	Transactions incidental to the foreign exchange activities undertaken by these institutions.
Full Fledged Money Changers (FFMCs)	• Dept. of Posts • Urban Co-op. Banks • Other FFMCs	Purchase of foreign exchange and sale for private and business visits abroad.

CHAPTER 5
TREASURY

I.   INTRODUCTION

Treasury, as the name suggests, takes care of funds of the bank. Treasury is defined in Webster Dictionary as "a place where stores of treasures are kept; the place of deposit, care, and disbursement of collected funds". Its role is very important in every organization. But the importance is all the more in banks as the bank's primary function is to deal in money.

Banks accept deposit at a lower cost to lend at higher cost; the difference being their gross margin out of which they meet their expenses, bear cost of risk taken to lend and earn balance as profit. The sources of funds are broadly their own capital and savings, current and fixed deposit from public. The deployment of funds is in fixed assets of the bank and in loans/advances to public. This entire activity of generating funds and deployment is carried out from network of branches. It requires pooling of resources at one place and then deploying from various places. Treasury is the pooling point.

Besides, while the deposits are payable on demand or at different points of time, the lending is having altogether different repayment profile. Only a few depositors would withdraw their deposit at any given point of time. Therefore, banks are able to lend major part of the deposit while keeping balance as liquid to meet such demand. If the balance on hand is less than demand, banks will have a problem in repaying the demanded amount. On the other hand, if banks excess amount in hand, they don't earn any amount on it and hence incur loss.

This fine tuning of demand and supply is done by the Treasury. RBI, as regulator, keeps a close watch on this to ensure that banks don't default on this. There are statutory obligations on the part of the banks to have a minimum amount in the form of cash (called Cash Reserve Ratio - CRR) and also a minimum investment in liquid securities (called Statutory Liquidity Ratio – SLR). It is the responsibility of the Treasury of the bank to ensure that these ratios are maintained on day-to-day basis.

In short, deposits received at branches and all money lent by branches are pooled and routed through the Treasury which has to ensure that minimum cash and liquid is kept in hand to meet banks' obligations to their customers, apart from meeting statutory CRR and SLR ratios as stipulated by RBI.

Further, banks provide foreign exchange services to their customers – importers/exporters, non-resident Indians, residents going abroad etc. This results in sale and purchase of various foreign currencies from different branches. This again is through pooling of sale and purchase outflow/inflow at Treasury. The responsibility rests with the Treasury to make available required foreign currency and deploy excess amount in the market. The Treasury buys and sells foreign currency, like any other commodity, in the foreign exchange market. In addition, it creates a network of foreign correspondent banks to facilitate foreign exchange transactions of the customers and to keep balance of foreign exchange to meet requirements.

In addition, Treasury provides different rupee and foreign exchange products/services like derivatives, swaps, remittance facilities etc. to customers.

Banks also at times trade in stock market/money market/foreign exchange market to maximize returns on investments. This activity is also taken care of by the Treasury.

II.   ROLE AND RESPONSIBILITIES

It would be seen from the aforesaid that Treasury plays a pivotal role in managing funds in the bank. In the process, it is exposed to various risks like liquidity, interest rate, exchange, credit and operational risks. Efficient functioning of the treasury is therefore imperative for a bank.

The aforesaid activities of Treasury can be broadly categorized in following 3 roles:

a.   Liquidity Management: Treasury is responsible to ensure that the bank meets statutory Cash Reserve Requirements (CRR) and Statutory Liquidity Ratio (SLR) on day to day basis along with meeting funds requirements to meet customer demands.

b.   Risk Management: Treasury provides necessary inputs to management to take appropriate policy and strategic decisions to manage risks – interest rate risk, asset liability mismatch risk (ALM), exchange risk, market risk, credit risk, operational risks etc.

c. Proprietary Book management: Treasury may trade in currencies, securities and other financial instruments, including derivatives, in consonance with the regulatory provisions and banks' policies in order to contribute to Bank's profits

III.   FUNCTIONS

The functions of Treasury have been explained in the following paragraphs.

i)   Foreign Exchange Market

a.   Sale & Purchase of foreign currency

Banks handle foreign exchange business of its clients for which they buy/sell foreign exchange and maintain foreign currency balances in banks abroad. In addition, they trade in foreign currency for its own book as well within the laws and regulations prevailing in the country to earn income.

In India, Reserve Bank of India (RBI) has been empowered under Foreign Exchange Management Act to authorize persons/legal entities ("Authorized Dealers") to undertake the business of foreign exchange. Most of the banks are Authorized Dealers to deal in foreign exchange to cater to the foreign exchange needs of their clients engaged in export and import trade in respect of majority of world currencies like U S Dollar, Sterling Pounds, Euro, Swiss Francs, and Japanese Yen etc. They also render services of hedging of foreign currency risks by providing forward covers and various derivative products. For Non-Resident Indians, banks provide remittance facilities and acceptance of deposits in Indian Rupees (NRE / NRO) as well as in designated foreign currencies (FCNR).

b. Currency Position Management

Banks are required to maintain foreign currency balances to be able to effect buying/selling of foreign exchange on behalf of their clients. For exports by their clients, they receive foreign currency and for imports they have to pay in foreign currency. Similarly, in case of inward remittance from NRIs, they receive foreign currency. If they do not keep balance in foreign currency, they lose out on the exchange rate profits.

All these activities require maintenance of balances in foreign currency accounts which needs close supervision. Moreover, there are regulatory requirements to keep these balances within permissible limits.

This activity of managing Currency Position is one of the most critical activities that Treasury undertakes.

c. Forward Cover

Forward Cover is booked to manage foreign exchange rate risk in a transaction in which foreign currency is receivable at a future date. To freeze the exchange rate, the buyer/ seller takes a forward cover to buy/sell the currency on a future date at a fixed rate. In this transaction, the money does not actually change hands until the agreed upon future date, and the transaction occurs on that date, regardless of what the market rates are then. The duration of the trade can be one day, a few days, months or years. Usually, the date is decided by both parties. Then the forward contract is negotiated and agreed upon by both parties.

d. Derivatives

Derivative is defined as an Instrument, to be settled at a future date, whose value is derived from change in interest rate, foreign exchange rate, credit rating or credit index, price of securities (also called "underlying"), or any other underlying or a combination of more than one of them and includes interest rate swaps, forward rate agreements, foreign currency swaps, foreign currency rupee swaps, foreign currency options, foreign currency rupee options etc. Some of these derivates are briefly explained below:

- Swaps

In this, two parties exchange currencies for a certain length of time and agree to reverse the transaction at a later date. These are not standardized contracts and are not traded through an exchange.

- Futures

Foreign currency futures are exchange traded forward transactions with standard contract sizes and maturity dates — for example, $1000 for next November at an agreed rate. Futures are standardized and are usually traded on an exchange created for this purpose. The average contract length is roughly 3 months. Futures contracts are usually inclusive of any interest amounts.

- Option

A foreign exchange option (commonly shortened to just FX option) is a derivative where the owner has the right but not the obligation to exchange money denominated in one currency into another currency at a pre-agreed exchange rate on a specified date. The FX options market is the deepest, largest and most liquid market for options of any kind in the world.

- Currency and Cross Currency Swaps

A 'Currency Swap' is a contract which commits two counterparties to exchange, over an agreed period, two streams of interest payments in different currencies, and at the end of the period to exchange the corresponding principal amounts at an exchange rate agreed to at the start of the contract. The principal amounts are also exchanged at the prevailing spot rate on inception.

The two streams of interest payments can be fixed/fixed, fixed/floating, floating/fixed or floating/floating.

Unlike an interest rate swap, the principal and interest are usually both exchanged in full in a currency swap.

A swap is referred to as 'cross-currency' when it involves an exchange of two streams of interest payments in different currencies, where at least one stream is at a floating rate of interest.

- Interest Rate Swap

A Single Currency Interest Rate Swap (IRS) is an exchange of cash flows between two counter parties at predetermined specifications. It is an obligation between them for exchange of interest payments or receipts on investments, in the same currency on an agreed amount of notional principal at regular intervals, over an agreed period of time. There are primarily two types of IRS –

- — Fixed to Floating - In this type of a swap the customer receives cash flows at a fixed rate of interest and simultaneously pays cash flows at a floating rate of interest or vice versa. The cash flows are calculated on a Notional Principal amount. The floating rate of interest is usually determined by reference to a transparent benchmark.

— Floating to Floating - In this kind of a swap, both the counter-parties exchange interest amounts based on two different floating reference rates, through the life of the swap

- <u>Forward Rate Arrangement</u>

A Forward Rate Agreement (FRA) is a contract where the parties agree that an interest rate (contract rate) will apply to a certain notional principal during a specified future period of time. An FRA is generally settled in cash at the beginning of the forward period.

A Forward Rate Agreement (FRA) is a cash-settled forward contract on a short-term loan. For example, a 3×9 FRA is a 3-month forward on a 6-month loan—the loan commences in 3 months and matures in 9. The interest rate on the loan—called the FRA rate—is set when the contract is first entered into. Because they are cash settled, no loan is ever extended. Instead, the contracts settle with a single cash payment linked to Libor (or Euribor).

e. **Payment Processing**

Payments between banks are looked after by Treasury. Banks make payments to other banks on behalf of their customers. Banks also receive payments from other banks for credit to their customer accounts. The processing of payments requires setting up inter-bank relationships/accounts. Treasury looks after these arrangements – both for domestic as well as international payments. The funding of these accounts and utilizing excess funds in these accounts require day-to-day monitoring. Treasury handles these activities.

- SWIFT Alliance

Inter-bank financial transactions are mostly routed through structured financial messaging system provided by SWIFT. The alliance with SWIFT is looked after by Treasury.

- Limit and Facility Monitoring

Banks extend foreign currency loans to their clients for which banks borrow in the market and surplus balances are lent in foreign markets. To facilitate this, banks set up correspondent banking arrangements with other banks which require monitoring on day-to-day basis and renewals from time to time. These arrangements may, inter-alia, also have credit lines on each other. These limits and facilities are subject to various terms and conditions. Treasury owns the responsibility for the entire Limit and Facility Monitoring in respect thereof.

Indian Scenario

Exchange rates in India are dependent upon market dynamics of demand and supply. The flow of foreign exchange is controlled/regulated by the Government of India through restrictions on imports/exports, capital inflow/outflow, external commercial borrowings and interest on foreign debt etc. In exceptional situation, sometimes, government through RBI enters into open market operations to stabilize the conditions. In other words, as far as foreign exchange market is concerned, it discovers price of each currency as per its own dynamics of demand and supply. But the government regulates demand and supply in the wider context of the economic and political considerations.

The capital account inflows/outflows are not free; permitted in a controlled way through FDI/FII guidelines. Limited free outflow has been permitted in the recent past by permitting individuals to take foreign exchange out for various purposes, including investment

Banks are allowed to maintain foreign exchange balances to meet their business requirements. Banks are also allowed to raise foreign debt for onward lending to their customers. Government has fixed upper limits for payment of interest on foreign debt.

Capital inflow by way of Foreign Direct Investment is controlled through FDI policy which defines type of investment, extent of investment and period of investment. The capital inflow in stock market is largely unrestricted but under close watch of SEBI.

To sum up:

- Foreign Exchange rates are uncontrolled

- Foreign Exchange inflows are regulated through –

  - Import/Export Trade policies

  - Capital Account Convertibility restrictions

  - Foreign Debt controls on amount and interest rate

  - Foreign Direct Investment controls

–   Capital Market Investment regulation

The Foreign Exchange Market is dominated by London, New York, Tokyo, Hong Kong, Singapore and Frankfurt. These markets are in different time zones and therefore market is practically open 24 hours for trading. Banks in India operate in these and other foreign exchange markets as per their requirement in each currency and settlement arrangement entered into by them.

The foreign exchange debt in India is linked to LIBOR (London Interbank Offered Rate). LIBOR is calculated and published daily by Thomson Reuters on behalf of the British Bankers' Association. It is a trimmed average of inter-bank deposit rates offered by designated contributor banks, for maturities ranging from overnight to one year. LIBOR is calculated for 10 currencies. There are either eight, twelve or sixteen contributor banks on each currency panel and the reported interest is the mean of the middle values. The rates are a benchmark reference rate for Pound Sterling and other currencies, including USD, Euro, Japanese Yen, Swiss Franc, Canadian Dollar etc. The interest rate ceiling on External Commercial Borrowing, stipulated by Government of India is also linked to LIBOR.

ii) Domestic Money Market

a. Call Money Market

Treasury manages all cash requirements of the bank across its branches as well as with RBI. It is the pooling point for all surpluses and the CRR requirement is managed on on-going basis. Requirements of branches are taken care of by Treasury by creating enough liquidity by borrowing in Call Money Market or by selling debt securities whenever required. Surplus is lent in the Call Money market (known as Call Borrowing/Lending or Overnight Inter-bank borrowing). This helps banks to manage their day-to-day shortfall/excess. The rates are driven by demand and supply.

b. Repo and Reverse Repo

RBI allows banks to borrow through Repo i.e., against pledge of securities for short periods. Banks borrow through Repo auction, where RBI purchases securities from banks with an agreement to sell back the securities after a fixed period. The difference in sale and purchase prices constitutes interest received by RBI.

Reverse Repo is lending of funds by banks to RBI in similar manner.

c. Collat. Borrowing & Lending Obligation

Collateralized Borrowing & Lending Obligation (CBLO) is a money market instrument launched by Clearing Corporation of India Ltd. (CCIL). CBLO is essentially a Repo instrument, which is used not only by banks and primary dealers, but also by all other players like financial institutions, insurance companies, mutual funds and corporates who cannot access call money market. CCIL acts as an intermediary.

d. Open Market Operations by RBI

RBI sells/buys government securities to control liquidity in the market and to influence the interest rates. RBI may absorb liquidity by selling the securities in the market and may infuse liquidity by buying back the securities from the public. These are known as open market operations (OMO) of the central bank.

e. Investment Management

It refers to sale/purchase of government securities/ approved debt securities by banks. Banks invest medium term surpluses in debt securities pending deployment in normal lending activity of the bank. These securities are subject to interest rate fluctuations and accordingly their market price keeps changing on day-to-day basis. Banks invest for meeting SLR obligations and also to invest surplus funds pending deployment as loans. The securities to be held till maturity are not required to be marked to the market price. But all other securities are marked to the market and therefore require active management. Treasury looks after all investments in securities.

The investment is done through Negotiated Dealing System (an electronic platform) set up by RBI for facilitating dealing in government securities and money market instruments. The NDS membership is open to banks, primary dealers, mutual funds, financial institutions and insurance companies. The clearing/settlement is handled by Clearing Corporation of India Ltd. (CCIL).

Apart from management of funds and liquidity, the domestic operations involve handling of financial instruments like:

• Commercial Papers

Commercial Paper is a short term borrowing instrument which corporates use to raise funds from market. It is mostly subscribed to by banks. The CP activities are regulated by RBI. It requires rating from a reputed Rating Agency. It is an unsecured instrument carrying promise from the corporate to pay the amount on a specified date to the payee. It is transferable by endorsement and it is traded in the money market. It attracts stamp duty.

- Certificate of Deposits

CD is a kind of "term deposit" issued by banks. It is a transferable paper and attracts stamp duty. While fixed deposits cannot be transferred, CD can be transferred to others. It is in the form of promissory note and is issued at a discount to face value. Loan against security of CD is not permitted. Payment before maturity is not allowed.

- Government Securities

These are securities which are notified by the Government as approved securities for investment by banks for considering them under SLR category.

- Treasury Bills

RBI raises funds from the money market by issuing Treasury Bills. These instruments are backed by government guarantee for payment on maturity. These instruments are issued by RBI for meeting funds requirements of the government.

- Bonds and Debentures

These are debt instruments mostly raised by public and private sector companies. Banks invest in these instruments to park their surplus funds pending deployment in the lending activity. While income on these bonds and debentures is not as remunerative as normal lending, the investment in these instruments provides liquidity and an avenue for quick entry and exit when required. This being market activity, is undertaken by the Treasury.

- Equities

Exposure to Equity market is not a normal business of a bank. However, banks have permission to have a limited exposure (around 5%) in the stock market. Banks generally acquire these shares as security or through direct intervention in the market for strategic purposes. The investment in stock market and/or buying/selling is handled by the Treasury.

- Derivatives

Banks mostly undertake derivative activities on behalf of their customers like Interest Rate Swap (IRS) and Forward Rate Arrangement (FRA).

iii) Liquidity Management & Reg. Compliance

Treasury is responsible for all regulatory compliances with respect to CRR, SLR, ALM, FEMA guidelines etc. Liquidity management means ensuring that bank is liquid enough to honor its business liabilities as well as statutory liabilities – CRR, SLR, position maintenance etc. All these activities converge at Treasury.

Treasury is also responsible to ensure that applicable accounting standards for securities as well as derivatives in respect of money market and foreign exchange are strictly complied with as per laid down rules and regulations.

iv) Statutory and Management Reporting

Banks have a host of regulatory reporting and compliance responsibilities like CRR, SLR, Foreign Exchange Position, Asset Liability Management, Trading Position etc. Besides, bank management requires a host of reports on regulatory compliances as well as on management of funds. Treasury manages close to 40% of total resources of the bank. Efficient working of Treasury requires close monitoring and strategic decision making on on-going basis. Treasury provides necessary inputs to the management.

IV. ORGANIZATIONAL STRUCTURE

Bank Treasuries generally have following departments/ sections to perform aforementioned roles:

- Fixed Income or Money Market Division, which handles debt instruments. Fixed income refers to any type of investment that yields a regular (or fixed) return.

- Foreign Exchange Division which handles foreign currency transactions

- Capital Market Division which deals in shares listed on the stock market

- Proprietary Trading desk that conducts trading activities for the bank's own account

- Asset Liability Management (ALM) desk to manage interest rate and liquidity mismatch. Banks manage the risks of Asset Liability mismatch by matching the assets and liabilities according to the maturity pattern or the matching the duration through strategic product pricing, hedging and securitization etc.

- Desk to formulate Transfer Pricing for different business segments

As is evident from the aforesaid, the activities of treasury require on-line link with money market and foreign exchange market. Banks are linked to the domestic market (inter-bank money market, Clearing Corporation of India, Stock Market, and Negotiated Dealing System etc.) through dedicated on-line interface. For foreign exchange transactions, banks are linked to international markets – London/US/Hong Kong etc. where various currencies are traded, with suitable settlement mechanism.

Front Office has dealers who are provided with on-line access to these markets through dedicated terminals. They are empowered to buy/sell on-line as per requirements within their defined powers. The dealers are the front end for counter parties for all practical purposes and the contracts entered into by the dealers are binding on the bank.

The Mid Office is involved in limit management, deal verification and risk management on on-line basis. In other words, if front office is the "Maker" of the deal, mid office is the "Checker" of the deal. This ensures that the transactions are under dual control. Though mid office "checking" is concurrent, it is not a prior authorization. The front office dealer concludes the deals where after it comes to mid office for verification/regulation etc., concurrently.

Back Office takes care of the operational aspects of the deal like accounting, effecting payment, maintaining balance, reporting etc.

Most of the large banks have installed automated dealing systems for on-line transactions and seamless flow of information between front office, mid office and back office. These banks have integrated all treasury functions under one roof to have an enterprise level view on various risks as they have realized that interest risk, credit risk, market risk and liquidity risk are inter-related.

To recapitulate, functions of the aforesaid 3 sections of the treasury are as under:

i)   **Front Office**

Front Office dealing operations include:

—   Real time position management, monitoring and display;

—   Integrated limit checking;

—   Intuitive, streamlined deal entry function, for the required instrument set.

ii) **Middle Office**

Middle Office functionality includes:

—   Deal verification & approval workflow operations;

—   Limit management & analysis (including VaR limit support);

—   Real time risk management tools, including mark-to-market (for all supported instruments), VaR derivation (Delta-Gamma), scenario analysis, NPV derivation.

— Control & auditing support.

iii) Back Office

Back Office processing includes the following functions:

— Deal Confirmation production and matching control (using electronic systems such as SWIFT Accord & Misys Treasury Plus, & manual paper based processes where required);

— Deal settlement, including payment / wire management directly with banks and via SWIFT MT 1xx/2xx/3xx & 540 series messaging;

— Accounting, including Nostro accounting and journal creation and export as required;

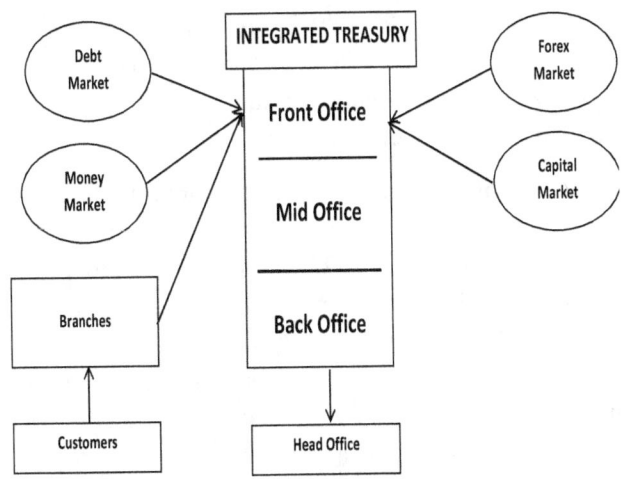

Automatic generation of operational and management reporting. Multiple roles necessitate Treasury to manage an ALM Book for internal risk management, a Merchant Book for client-related currency and derivative transactions, and a Trading Book for managing its proprietary positions. ALM Book also includes traditional role of Treasury in liquidity management.

Treasury, as the name suggests, takes care of funds of the bank. Treasury is defined in Webster Dictionary as "a place where stores of treasures are kept; the place of deposit, care, and disbursement of collected funds". Its role is very important in every organisation. But the importance is all the more in banks as the bank's primary function is to deal in money. Banks accept deposit to lend. It requires pooling of resources at one place and then deploying from various places. Treasury is the pooling point. While banks lend the money taken as deposit, they have to keep enough liquidity to meet repayment demand from depositors. Therefore, banks keep a portion of the deposit as liquid to meet such demand. If the balance in liquid form is less than the demand, banks will have a problem in repayment. On the other hand, if banks keep excess liquid amount in hand, they don't earn any amount on it and hence incur loss.

This fine tuning of demand and supply is done by the Treasury. RBI, as regulator, keeps a close watch on this to ensure that banks don't default. Banks have statutory obligation to maintain a minimum amount in the form of cash called Cash Reserve Ratio - CRR and also a minimum investment in approved liquid securities called Statutory Liquidity Ratio – SLR. It is the responsibility of the Treasury of the bank to ensure that these ratios are maintained on day-to-day basis.

In short, deposits received at branches and all money lent by branches are pooled and routed through the Treasury which has to ensure that minimum cash and liquidity is kept in hand to meet bank's obligations to their customers, apart from meeting statutory CRR and SLR ratios as stipulated.

Treasury deploys funds sourced by Branches in the form of deposits i.e., the net funds that are left after lending and meeting cash requirements, in the market by way of investment. Branches are compensated for their contribution of funds by way of transfer pricing. In the process, Treasury generates some net income for itself.

Besides this activity, treasury manages foreign exchange activity of the bank. Banks provide foreign exchange services to their customers – importers/exporters, non-resident Indians, residents going abroad etc. This results in sale and purchase of different foreign currencies from customers at branches. The management of currency risks arising out of this activity is undertaken through pooling of sale and purchase of foreign currency transactions, outflows/inflows etc. The responsibility rests with the Treasury to make available required foreign currency and deploy excess amount in the market. Treasury buys and sells foreign currency, like any other commodity, in the foreign exchange market. In addition, it creates a network of foreign correspondent banks to facilitate foreign exchange transactions of the customers and to keep balance of foreign exchange to meet requirements.

Further, Treasury provides different rupee and foreign exchange products and services like derivatives, swaps, remittance facilities etc. to customers. This fetches fee income to the bank.

Banks also, at times, trade in stock market/money market/foreign exchange market to maximise returns on investments. This is called bank's 'Proprietary Trading' function and is subject to strict regulatory compliance and limits setup by respective bank's board. This activity is also taken care of by the Treasury.

It would be seen from the aforesaid that Treasury plays a pivotal role in managing funds in domestic currency and in foreign exchange. In the process, it has to manage various risks like liquidity, interest rate, exchange, credit and operations risks.

i) Role and Responsibilities

The responsibilities of the Treasury can be broadly categorised as under:

a. Liquidity Management

   Treasury is responsible for ensuring that the bank meets prescribed Cash Reserve Ratio (CRR) and Statutory Liquidity Ratio (SLR) obligations on day-to-day basis along with funding requirements to meet customer demands.

b. Risk Management

   Treasury provides necessary inputs to management to take appropriate policy and strategic decisions to manage risks – interest rate risk, asset liability mismatch risk, exchange risk, market risk, credit risk, operations risk etc.

c. Proprietary Book Management.

d. Trade in currencies, securities and other financial instruments, including derivatives.

The Role of Treasury is broadly explained in the following diagram.

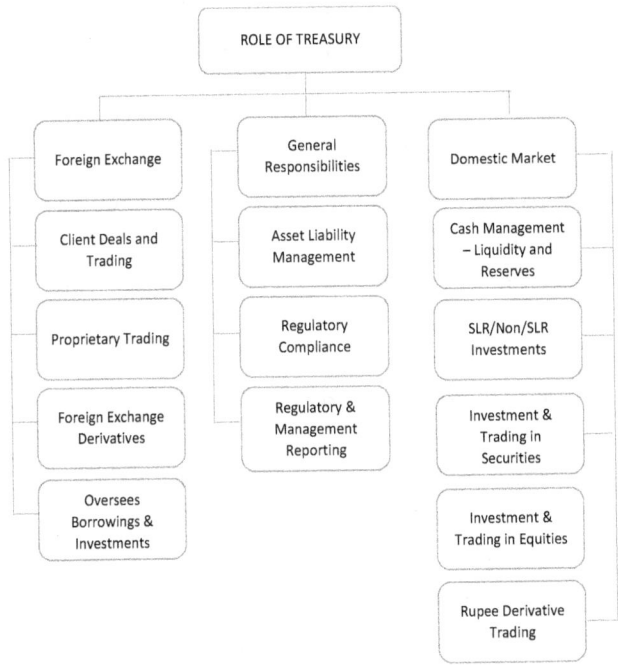

ii) Functions

a. Call Money Market Operations

b. Repo and Reverse Repo Operations

c. Collateralized Borrowing and Lending Obligation (CBLO) Operations

d. Sale & Purchase of foreign currency

e. Currency Position Management

f. Forward Cover – sale/purchase of foreign currency on a future date at pre-fixed rates

g. Derivatives such as Futures, Option, Currency and Cross Currency Swaps, Interest Rate Swap, Forward Rate Agreement (FRA)

h. Banks make payments to other banks on behalf of their customers. Banks also receive payments from other banks for credit to their customer accounts. The processing of payments requires setting up inter-bank relationships/accounts. Treasury looks after these arrangements – both for domestic as well as international payments. The funding of these accounts and utilizing excess funds in these accounts require day-to-day monitoring. Treasury handles these activities.

i. SWIFT Alliance – Inter-bank financial transactions are mostly routed through structured financial messaging system provided by SWIFT. The alliance with SWIFT is looked after by Treasury.

j. Limit and Facility Monitoring - Banks extend foreign currency loans to their clients and for that purpose banks borrow in the market and surplus balances are lent in market. To facilitate this, banks set up correspondent banking arrangements with other banks which require monitoring on day-to-day basis and renewals from time to time. These arrangements may, inter-alia, have credit lines on each other. These limits and facilities are subject to various terms and conditions. Treasury owns the responsibility for the entire Limit and Facility Monitoring in respect thereof.

k. Investment Management – Banks invest in various types of financial instruments such as Government

Securities, Treasury Bills, Bonds, Debentures, Commercial Papers, Certificate of Deposits. Equities, Derivatives.

l. Liquidity Management and Regulatory Compliance – Treasury is responsible for all regulatory compliances with respect to CRR, SLR, ALM, FEMA guidelines etc. Liquidity management means ensuring that bank is liquid enough to honor its business liabilities as well as statutory liabilities – CRR, SLR, position maintenance etc. All these activities converge at Treasury. Treasury is also responsible to ensure that applicable accounting standards for securities as well as derivatives in respect of money market and foreign exchange are strictly complied with as per laid down rules and regulations.

m. Statutory and Management Reporting – Bank management requires a host of reports on regulatory compliances like CRR, SLR, Foreign Exchange Position, Trading Position etc. It also requires reporting in respect of Asset Liability Management and management of funds. Treasury manages close to 40% of total resources of the bank. Efficient working of Treasury requires close monitoring and strategic decision making on an on-going basis. Treasury provides necessary inputs to the management.

Multiple roles make it necessary for Treasury to manage an ALM Book for internal risk management, a Merchant Book for client-related currency and derivative transactions, and a Trading Book for managing its proprietary positions. ALM Book also includes traditional role of Treasury in liquidity management.

iii) Organizational Structure

In order to manage these functions, the activities are divided into front office, mid office and back office. Broad overview of the activities of each of these offices is given below:

a. Front Office

Front Office has dealers who are provided with on-line access to these markets through dedicated terminals. They are empowered to buy/sell on-line as per requirements within their defined powers. The dealers are the front end for counter parties for all practical purposes and the contracts entered into by the dealers are binding on the bank.

b. Mid Office

The Mid Office is involved in limit management, deal verification and risk management etc. on on-line basis. Front Office dealer concludes the deals where after it comes to mid office. Mid Office functionality includes -

- Setting up various limits and workflow processes.

- Limit management and analysis including Value at Risk (VaR) limit support.

- Real time risk management tools, including mark-to-market, VaR derivation (Delta-Gamma), scenario analysis and NPV derivation etc.

- Control and auditing support.

c. Back Office

Back Office takes care of the operational aspects of the deal like accounting, effecting payment, maintaining balance, reporting etc. Back Office processing includes the following functions -

- Deal verification and ensuring workflow of operations.

- Deal confirmation, issuing deal ticket and counterparty matching control using electronic systems such as SWIFT Accord and Misys Treasury Plus and manual paper based processes wherever required.

- Deal settlement, including payment and wire management directly with banks and via SWIFT MT 1xx/2xx/3xx and 540 series messaging.

- Accounting, including Nostro accounting and journal creation.

- Automatic generation of operational and management reporting